HOMER'S
THE ODYSSEY

Other books in the Christian Guides
to the Classics Series:

Bunyan's "The Pilgrim's Progress"

Dickens's "Great Expectations"

Hawthorne's "The Scarlet Letter"

Milton's "Paradise Lost"

Shakespeare's "Macbeth"

HOMER'S
THE ODYSSEY

LELAND RYKEN

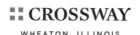
WHEATON, ILLINOIS

Homer's "The Odyssey"

Copyright © 2013 by Leland Ryken

Published by Crossway
    1300 Crescent Street
    Wheaton, Illinois 60187

Cover illustration: Howell Golson

Cover design: Simplicated Studio

First printing 2013

Printed in the United States of America

Unless otherwise indicated, Scripture quotations are from the ESV® Bible (*The Holy Bible, English Standard Version®*), copyright © 2001 by Crossway. 2011 Text Edition. Used by permission. All rights reserved.

Trade paperback ISBN: 978-1-4335-2616-9
PDF ISBN: 978-1-4335-2617-6
Mobipocket ISBN: 978-1-4335-2618-3
ePub ISBN: 978-1-4335-2619-0

Library of Congress Cataloging-in-Publication Data

Ryken, Leland.
  Homer's The Odyssey / Leland Ryken.
    p. cm.— (Christian guides to the classics)
    ISBN 978-1-4335-2616-9 (tp)
    1. Homer. Odyssey. 2. Christianity and literature. 3. Epic poetry, Greek—History and criticism. 4. Odysseus (Greek mythology) in literature. I. Title.
PA4167.R94   2013
883'.01—dc23   2012025867

Crossway is a publishing ministry of Good News Publishers.

BP		22	21	20	19	18	17	16	15	14	13
15	14	13	12	11	10	9	8	7	6	5	4	3	2	1

Contents

The Nature and Function of Literature

We need to approach any piece of writing with the right expectations, based on the kind of writing that it is. The expectations that we should bring to any work of literature are the following.

The subject of literature. The subject of literature is human experience, rendered as concretely as possible. Literature should thus be contrasted to expository writing of the type we use to conduct the ordinary business of life. Literature does not aim to impart facts and information. It exists to make us share a series of experiences. Literature appeals to our image-making and image-perceiving capacity. A famous novelist said that his purpose was to make his readers *see*, by which he meant to see life.

The universality of literature. To take that one step further, the subject of literature is *universal* human experience—what is true for all people at all times in all places. This does not contradict the fact that literature is first of all filled with concrete particulars. The particulars of literature are a net whereby the author captures and expresses the universal. History and the daily news tell us what *happened*; literature tells us what *happens*. The task that this imposes on us is to recognize and name the familiar experiences that we vicariously live as we read a work of literature. The truth that literature imparts is truthfulness to life—knowledge in the form of seeing things accurately. As readers we not only look *at* the world of the text but *through* it to everyday life.

An interpretation of life. In addition to portraying human experiences, authors give us their interpretation of those experiences. There is a persuasive aspect to literature, as authors attempt to get us to share their views of life. These interpretations of life can be phrased as ideas or themes. An important part of assimilating imaginative literature is thus determining and evaluating an author's angle of vision and belief system.

The importance of literary form. A further aspect of literature arises from the fact that authors are artists. They write in distinctly literary genres such as narrative and poetry. Additionally, literary authors want us to share their love of technique and beauty, all the way from skill with words to an ability to structure a work carefully and artistically.

Summary. A work of imaginative literature aims to make us see life accurately, to get us to think about important ideas, and to enjoy an artistic performance.

Why the Classics Matter

This book belongs to a series of guides to the literary classics of Western literature. We live at a time when the concept of a literary classic is often misunderstood and when the classics themselves are often undervalued or even attacked. The very concept of a classic will rise in our estimation if we simply understand what it is.

What is a classic? To begin, the term *classic* implies the best in its class. The first hurdle that a classic needs to pass is excellence. Excellent according to whom? This brings us to a second part of our definition: classics have stood the test of time through the centuries. The human race itself determines what works rise to the status of classics. That needs to be qualified slightly: the classics are especially known and valued by people who have received a formal education, alerting us that the classics form an important part of the education that takes place within a culture.

This leads us to yet another aspect of classics: classics are known to us not only in themselves but also in terms of their interpretation and reinterpretation through the ages. We know a classic partly in terms of the attitudes and interpretations that have become attached to it through the centuries.

Why read the classics? The first good reason to read the classics is that they represent the best. The fact that they are difficult to read is a mark in their favor; within certain limits, of course, works of literature that demand a lot from us will always yield more than works that demand little of us. If we have a taste for what is excellent, we will automatically want some contact with classics. They offer more enjoyment, more understanding about human experience, and more richness of ideas and thought than lesser works (which we can also legitimately read). We finish reading or rereading a classic with a sense of having risen higher than we would otherwise have risen.

Additionally, to know the classics is to know the past, and with that knowledge comes a type of power and mastery. If we know the past, we are in some measure protected from the limitations that come when all we know is the contemporary. Finally, to know the classics is to be an educated person. Not to know them is, intellectually and culturally speaking, like walking around without an arm or leg.

Summary. Here are four definitions of a literary classic from literary experts; each one provides an angle on why the classics matter. (1) The best that has been thought and said (Matthew Arnold). (2) "A literary classic ranks with the best of its kind that have been produced" (*Harper Handbook to Literature*). (3) A classic "lays its images permanently on the mind [and] is entirely irreplaceable in the sense that no other book whatever comes anywhere near reminding you of it or being even a momentary substitute for it" (C. S. Lewis). (4) Classics are works to which "we return time and again in our minds, even if we do not reread them frequently, as touchstones by which we interpret the world around us" (Nina Baym).

How to Read a Story

The Odyssey, like the other classics discussed in this series, is a narrative or story. To read it with enjoyment and understanding, we need to know how stories work and why people write and read them.

Why do people tell and read stories? To tell a story is to (a) entertain and (b) make a statement. As for the entertainment value of stories, it is a fact that one of the most universal human impulses can be summed up in the four words *tell me a story*. The appeal of stories is universal, and all of us are incessant storytellers during the course of a typical day. As for *making a statement*, a novelist hit the nail on the head when he said that in order for storytellers to tell a story they must have some picture of the world and of what is right and wrong in that world.

The things that make up a story. All stories are comprised of three things that claim our attention—setting, character, and plot. A good story is a balance among these three. In one sense, storytellers tell us *about* these things, but in another sense, as fiction writer Flannery O'Connor put it, storytellers don't speak *about* plot, setting, and character but *with* them. *About what* does the storyteller tell us by means of these things? About life, human experience, and the ideas that the storyteller believes to be true.

World making as part of storytelling. To read a story is to enter a whole world of the imagination. Storytellers construct their narrative world carefully. World making is a central part of the storyteller's enterprise. On the one hand, this is part of what makes stories entertaining. We love to be transported from mundane reality to faraway places with strange-sounding names. But storytellers also intend their imagined worlds as accurate pictures of reality. In other words, it is an important part of the truth claims that they intend to make. Accordingly, we need to pay attention to the details of the world that a storyteller creates, viewing that world as a picture of what the author believes to exist.

The need to be discerning. The first demand that a story makes on us is surrender—surrender to the delights of being transported, of encountering experiences, characters, and settings, of considering the truth claims that an author makes by means of his or her story. But we must not be morally and intellectually passive in the face of what an author puts before us. We need to be true to our own convictions as we weigh the morality and truth claims of a story. A story's greatness does not guarantee that it tells the truth in every way.

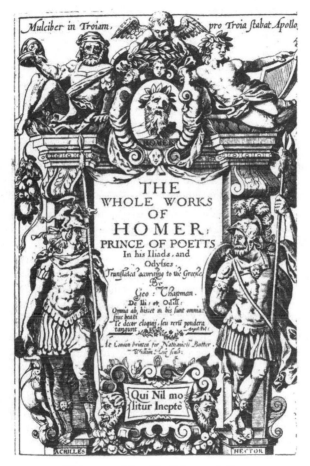

Title page of first English translation
(George Chapman, 1616)

The Odyssey: The Book at a Glance

Author. Legendary poet Homer

Nationality. Greek

Date of writing. Unknown

Approximate number of pages. 350 (varies from one translation to another)

Available editions. Modern translations abound; some names of translators and the publisher of each are as follows: W. H. D. Rouse (Signet); Edward McCrorie (Johns Hopkins University Press); Richmond Lattimore (Harper & Row); Allen Mandelbaum (Bantam); Robert Fitzgerald (Farrar, Straus & Giroux); Robert Fagles (Penguin)

Genres. Epic; myth; fantasy; hero story; adventure story; travel story

Setting for the story. The Mediterranean Sea and its coast, especially Ithaca (home of Odysseus), perhaps in the eleventh century BC (approximately contemporaneous with the Old Testament judges)

Main characters. Odysseus, protagonist of the story, whose journey to his home in Ithaca after the battle at Troy is the main action; Odysseus's wife, Penelope, who has waited for her husband to return from what becomes a twenty-year absence; a hundred villainous suitors who devour Odysseus's goods as they attempt to win Penelope as a wife; Telemachos, son of Odysseus, who comes of age during the course of the action; the goddess Athena (wisdom), who aids Odysseus in his ordeals; the god Poseidon, who instigates the trouble that Odysseus endures on his journey home

Plot summary. After fighting in the Trojan War for ten years, Odysseus sets sail for his home in Ithaca with a crew of shipmates. Poseidon pursues a grudge against Odysseus by making the sea voyage a continuous series of ordeals lasting ten years by the time Odysseus reaches home. After triumphing in a series of twelve adventures (which are also temptations and tests), Odysseus returns home, the only one of his men to survive. Odysseus joins forces with his son Telemachos to slaughter the suitors in the hall of his palace, after which Odysseus is reunited with his wife, Penelope.

The structure of the story. (1) Because a convention of epic is to begin *in medias res* (the Latin phrase meaning "in the middle of things"), the story line noted above gets rearranged in the actual plot of the story. *The Odyssey* has a firm, three-part plot: the Telemachia (Books 1–4, which narrate the travels of Telemachos to find his father and describe the disorder that has engulfed Odysseus's home in Ithaca); the wanderings of Odysseus (Books 5–12); the return or homecoming of Odysseus (Books 13–24, narrating what happened when Odysseus returns home). (2) The story is structured as a quest for the hero to return home. Like all quest stories, the story presents the hero with a series of obstacles that must be overcome before the quest can end successfully. (3) The story has a U-shaped comic plot in which events descend into tragedy but rise to a happy ending.

Cultural context. *The Odyssey* belongs to ancient classical culture, and it embodies the values that we call "classicism." One of these values is a human-centered focus known as humanism—the striving to perfect all human possibilities in this life. The ethical outlook is one that regards reason and intellect as the human faculties that lead to virtue. More specifically, classical ethics believed that it was the function of reason to control the emotions and appetites. There is no better illustration than the middle section of *The Odyssey*, where Odysseus is tempted to indulge his feelings and appetites and where ultimately his reason (partly represented by Athena, goddess of wisdom) is what rescues him from vice. Another facet of humanism is the urge for human action, exertion, and achievement.

The importance of Homer to the classical world. A modern scholar has offered the opinion that the important question regarding Homer is not *who* he was but *what* he was. *The Iliad* and *The Odyssey* were a kind of Bible to ancient Greeks. Plato in his *Republic* says that some Greek citizens thought that a person should regulate all of life according to what Homer said. Referring to Homer was a standard way to answer a philosophic or moral question. Professionals known as Homerids gave recitals of Homer accompanied by commentary.

Tips for reading. (1) An epic is a special kind of story, and the kind most governed by literary conventions (understood "rules" that a composer is expected to incorporate). These will be noted in the remainder of this book. The preliminary point to be made is that an epic storyteller expects readers to relish the specific version of an epic motif that he reenacts for their enjoyment. (2) Epics were originally oral performances. At the beginning of Book 9 of *The Odyssey* we are given an account of how an ancient epic was actually performed, and it is a picture of what we know as after-dinner entertainment. This means that we should read *The Odyssey* first of all for its entertainment value. (3) On the other hand, for the cultures who produced epics, an epic summed up what a whole age wanted to say. After enjoying the author's virtuosity in reenacting epic conventions, therefore, we need to ponder the world view and sense of life that the story embodies.

The Author and His Faith

Homer and his culture belong to what is commonly called paganism—a religious belief system that exists apart from Christian influence. At the heart of that religion is mythology. Strictly defined, a myth is a story about the gods, but by extension it refers to stories with a heavy reliance on the supernatural, even if some characters in the story might be superhuman rather than divine. We can say of Homer's worldview that it is religious in orientation, with the gods and goddesses playing a prominent role in human affairs.

Mythology as religion. After a mythological system such as Greek mythology ceases to be believed as an active religion, it becomes a purely literary phenomenon, which is what Homer's mythology is for modern readers. But as we read *The Odyssey* we need to assimilate it as Homer and his audience did—as a religious system. That religion was *polytheistic*, with dozens of gods and goddesses making up the pantheon ("all the gods") of Greek religion. The portrayal of these deities was thoroughly *anthropomorphic* (portraying deity in human form)—so anthropomorphic, in fact, that the gods and goddesses seem to be little more than amplified humans. It is important to know, therefore, that there is one essential feature of the gods and goddesses that sets them apart from humans: they are immortal. Once alerted to this, we can pick up numerous clues of it in Homer's story.

Did the Greeks really believe in these gods? Plato was scandalized by Homer's portrayal of the gods, believing it to be unbecoming of deity. G. K. Chesterton has written with good sense on the subject in *The Everlasting Man*, claiming that even in Greek antiquity the mythological stories were regarded as trailing off into the domain of fairy stories. Certainly people did not say, "I believe in Zeus," the way Christians recite the Apostles' Creed.

Pagan parallels to Christianity. A notable feature of Greek mythology is that it contains numerous parallels (called "analogues") to the Christian religion—stories about divine intervention in people's lives, for example, or a description of a paradisal garden and a realm of afterlife to which people go after they have died. G. K. Chesterton said that these analogues are purely human attempts to arrive at religious truth by means of the imagination alone. C. S. Lewis speaks of "good dreams" that God sent to the human race as a foreshadowing of the reality found in the Bible and in Christ. Renaissance historian Walter Ralegh called these myths "crooked images of some one true history"—fallen humanity's unaided and only partially true version of a history found in its accurate form in the Bible.

How common grace figures into the equation. An important Christian doctrine is the idea of common grace—the belief that God endows all people, whether Christian or not, with a capacity for the good, the true, and the beautiful. Within this framework, wherever Homer's thinking agrees with Christianity, Christians can affirm it.

The Odyssey as Epic

The Odyssey belongs to a small, elite group of stories known as epics. Epics are long narrative poems (though some translations print Homer's poems as prose). Epics are the most exalted kind of story, and they are accordingly written in what is called the "high style." Starting with Homer, moreover, all epics incorporate a set of conventional patterns or motifs. Some of these conventions will be noted in the running commentary that follows, but here are six epic features to note at the outset:

- Epics are hero stories in which the action is dominated by a central character who embodies (despite imperfections) the ideals of the author's culture.
- The plot focuses on an epic feat, which in classical epic is always a battle. The hero's main achievement is winning a battle and earning a kingdom as his reward. Within this framework, the hero is automatically a warrior.
- Accordingly, the value structure of classical epic elevates physical strength, skill in warfare, and earthly success to a position of supremacy.
- The setting of action in an epic is so broad that it goes by the name of "epic sweep." It encompasses the whole earth, a supernatural world, and the afterlife.
- The story material of epic is mythology—a story about gods and super-humans, with supernatural or marvelous events in abundance.
- Stylistic traits include epic similes (extended comparisons using the formula *like* or *as* and having the effect of doing justice to the exalted nature of the material); circumlocution or periphrasis (taking more words than necessary to express something); and epithets (titles for persons or things).

The World of *The Odyssey*

Whenever we read a story, we enter a whole world of the imagination. Knowing the main features of that world is a good organizing framework within which to assimilate the story. The leading features of the world of *The Odyssey* include the following:

- A *domestic world* in which home and family are elevated to the highest human values. Hospitality and loyalty to home and family are prime virtues.
- A *mythological world* in which some of the characters are gods and god-desses, in which some of the human characters perform superhuman

actions, and in which many of the events and settings are supernatural (more than earthly).

- A *heroic world* in which warriors perform feats of battle and are motivated by a desire for fame, success, and material prosperity.
- An *aristocratic world* in which the important characters belong to the ruling class (which is also a warrior class).

BOOK 1

What Went on in the House of Odysseus

Plot Summary

Every story begins with exposition, and so does *The Odyssey*. Homer begins by reenacting the epic ritual of invoking the muse and stating the epic theme (that is, story material). The action then begins with an epic council of the gods in which the gods and goddesses decide what to do in human affairs. As we listen to the deliberations, we get the background information that we need for the story to follow.

The divine council in Book 1 of *The Odyssey* is occasioned by the sorry situation of the epic hero. Odysseus has been held captive on the island of the goddess Calypso for seven years. Meanwhile, Penelope, wife of Odysseus, is besieged by suitors who want her to declare her husband dead and marry one of them. The decision reached by the council involves a twofold action: (1) Athena (goddess of wisdom) is assigned to go to Odysseus's home in Ithaca and nudge Odysseus's son Telemachos to go on a journey in search of his father; (2) Hermes, messenger of the gods in classical mythology, is dispatched to the island of Calypso to announce the verdict of the gods that Calypso must let Odysseus depart.

Commentary

Everything in this packed opening book is important, starting with the invocation (which is our entry into the story). Even the detail that this is the story *of a man* is important, since epics always

The titles for the successive books of *The Odyssey* are additions to Homer's text supplied by editors or translators. Some translations do not supply titles. The titles used in this guide are from the Rouse translation. Examples of what other translations provide for Book 1 are "Trouble at Home" and "Athene Visits Telemachus." It is also helpful to know that various translators spell some of the Greek names differently.

All formal public events begin with ritual. The more formal the occasion, the more abundant is the ritual that accompanies it. Homer's opening invocation to the muse (goddess of inspiration) is a ritual event—the expected way for an epic poet to begin his performance. We can profitably compare this formal ritual with the ritual beginning of an important ballgame or a wedding that uses the Anglican marriage ceremony. A sense of formality and importance accompany all such rituals, including the invocation to the muse at the beginning of an epic.

Starting with the Middle Ages, it has been customary to call stories about the Trojan War "the matter of Troy." That total collection of story material can be divided into subcategories, such as preparation for battle, the battle of Troy, and the sack [destruction] of Troy. *The Odyssey* belongs to the category of return stories—stories of Greek heroes who returned home after helping Menelaos win the war that he undertook to reclaim his wife, Helen.

For Christian readers, the first encounter with Homer's portrayal of the gods and goddesses surely comes as a shock. Initially it is hard to know what to make of these freakish creatures that are more human than divine and yet are referred to as deities. The best thing to do is accept that these gods and goddesses are the best that the Greek person on the street could muster in a conception of God. In the Bible we read about God's taking his place among the gods (e.g., Ps. 84:1), and about his being superior to those gods. The song of Moses asks rhetorically, "Who is like you, O LORD, among the gods?" (Ex. 15:11). Homer's portrayal of the gods gives substance to such claims.

focus on universal human experience. When this particular epic hero is said to be "never at a loss" (or something equivalent, depending on the translation), we are alerted to Odysseus's two leading traits—his cleverness and his resourcefulness in mastering every obstacle. When Odysseus is said to have traveled far, we know that we have embarked on a travel story—such a famous travel story that the word *odyssey* has become a synonym for a journey of discovery. Other motifs to unpack in the opening invocation are the ideas of enduring hardships (so extreme that all of Odysseus's sailing companions have died), and home as the object of highest devotion.

So many details pass before us in this opening book that the effect resembles an ever-changing kaleidoscope. One way to organize the material is to be aware that *The Odyssey* as a whole synthesizes five story lines: (1) the story of Telemachos's coming of age (being initiated into adulthood); (2) the story of Penelope and the suitors; (3) the story of Odysseus's wanderings; (4) the story of the gods (including their "family" squabbles); (5) the story of Odysseus's homecoming and revenge. As the kaleidoscope turns during our trek through Book 1, we can find references to all five threads of action.

Another way to make sense of Book 1 is to operate on the premise that Homer intends to begin by placing before us the goal of the quest that underlies the story as a whole. Exactly what is it that propels Odysseus to endure ten years of ordeals? Book 1 answers that question by picturing three things—a wife, a son, and a kingdom. Homer manages the description of these things in such a way as to assure us that they are (a) things of great value and (b) things in great danger. The world of *The Odyssey* is consistently portrayed as a world in crisis (itself an epic convention). In Book 1 we are made to *feel* what Odysseus's absence from his kingdom means.

Finally, this book of exposition introduces us to the main characters of the story, and their essential nature is laid out for us to view—faithful Penelope, immature Telemachos, the villainous suitors, the humanlike gods and goddesses. We also learn a lot about Odysseus, even though he does not enter the story directly until Book 5. This narrative strategy is known as the delayed entrance of the hero.

For Reflection or Discussion

First, the commentary above names things that can be traced in the text; exactly where and how do these motifs surface in Book 1? Second, part of the excitement of the opening chapter or book of any story is that it is the reader's initiation into what is to follow, with the result that we need to make a mental note of what grabs our attention. Additionally, the opening unit of any story is our introduction to things that will become increasingly important and familiar to us as we progress through the story, so we need to read with the same alertness and expectation that we experience when being introduced to an important person for the first time. Finally, Book 1 of *The Odyssey* assembles a gallery of memorable characters for us to observe; we need to start to assemble a mental profile for each one.

It is in the nature of storytelling that the primary business that is transacted in the early phases of the story is to introduce the reader to the world of the story and the details about the plot and characters that we need to know before the story can proceed. This early material is known as "exposition" ("explanation"). It would be wrong to start looking for themes and religious meanings at the outset of the story, and we should not feel guilty when we simply focus on the story as a story at this early point. The details that Homer gives us in Book 1 are the materials from which he will eventually mold the deeper meanings of his story.

To read any epic, including this one, we need to read in an awareness of the importance of literary archetypes. An archetype is a plot motif, character type, or image/setting that recurs throughout literature and life. Once we name the archetypes that are placed in front of us in a given passage, we have an organizing framework for knowing what is happening. For example, the unifying action in *The Odyssey* is the quest. Naming archetypes also allows us to relate the story we are reading to other stories we have read, thereby unifying our total experience of literature.

The overall archetype that governs the story of Telemachos is the initiation into adulthood. More specifically, Telemachos undertakes a perilous journey that will take him to places remote from his home and that will test him and add to his fund of experience. Our imaginations reach out to include Jacob and Joseph from the book of Genesis, Moses, Huckleberry Finn, Pip in Charles Dickens's *Great Expectations*, Manolin in Ernest Hemingway's *The Old Man and the Sea*, and many another.

How the Council Met in the Market-Place of Ithaca, and What Came of It

Plot Summary

Book 2 is a sequel to Book 1, where the last phase of action is Athena's visit to Ithaca with the mission to get the youthful Telemachos off the launching pad. In that passage, Athena gives Telemachos a twofold game plan—to call a town meeting at which he must tell the suitors to leave, and to undertake a secret journey from his island home to the mainland in search of his father. Book 2 begins with the first of these two actions. Telemachos calls a meeting at which he speaks boldly to the suitors. It achieves absolutely nothing: the suitors talk back to Telemachos and go right on devouring Odysseus's goods.

The second half of Book 2 consists of preparations for the secret nighttime departure from the island. A key moment occurs when Telemachos goes to his father's storehouse, giving us a glimpse of the goal of Odysseus's quest and journey.

Commentary

Book 1 was expository—an introduction to the ingredients of the world of the story that we need to have at our disposal before the action can begin. With those "givens" at our disposal, in Book 2 the plot conflicts begin to unfold. Of course a story as expansive as *The Odyssey* has multiple plot conflicts. One of five threads of action in *The Odyssey* is the story of Telemachos. Overall it is an initiation story—a coming of age as Telemachos makes the transition from adolescence to adulthood.

The key to Book 2 is to observe the double-sided picture of Telemachos the initiate. On the one hand, Homer manages the description in such a way as to show signs of Telemachos's mastery and growing maturity. On the other hand, the inexperienced young hero fails to achieve his goal when he calls a meeting designed to send the suitors packing.

For Reflection or Discussion

The focus of this book is Telemachos. What do we learn about him? What are the evidences of growing maturity? What are the signs that he does not yet measure up?

Why does the son of Odysseus receive so much attention in Homer's story? Ancient cultures placed extreme value on the idea of worthy sons. In this way of thinking, the quest of Odysseus will be partly thwarted if his son does not prove to be a worthy successor to him. The Old Testament book of Proverbs expresses this same view of worthy sons.

BOOK 3
What Happened in Sandy Pylos

Plot Summary

Book 2 ended on a note of high drama, with Telemachos setting out on a secret and dangerous nighttime journey with a crew of sailors. The journey that Telemachos undertakes is a fact-finding mission to learn about his father's whereabouts. The first leg of the journey is to the kingdom of Nestor, one of the Greek warriors who fought at Troy. Telemachos is welcomed into the court, where the conversation turns to Odysseus after the niceties of arrival (including dinner) have been observed.

At this point we need to understand and relish how professional epic storytellers go about their trade. Epic storytellers care little for plot suspense.

Probably the dominant impression that Book 3 leaves with us is the extreme details that the niceties of arrival and leave-taking receive. Homer seems never to tire of narrating the protocol that was observed whenever a traveling stranger arrived at a place or left it. There is a ready explanation for this: *The Odyssey* is a domestic epic, and hospitality is one of the highest values in such a world. Abraham and Sarah's entertainment of three angelic strangers (Gen. 18:1–8) is a biblical parallel.

Book 3 is our initiation into two activities that will recur throughout this epic. One is the practice of sacrifices to the gods, accompanied by prayers and gestures of reverence. The other is eating and drinking, which belong to the code of hospitality. In *The Odyssey*, one line in thirty concerns the preparation or consumption of food, or references to hunger and thirst. Additionally, these references to the physical needs of life are part of the realism for which Homer is famous.

In addition to repeated references in *The Odyssey* to the contrast between the homecomings of Agamemnon and Odysseus, we hear multiple times about the parallel between the sons of those two heroes. Agamemnon's son Orestes took quick and decisive vengeance on Aegisthos for killing his father; this is the implied standard to which Telemachos needs to measure up.

Instead they resort to foreshadowing, so that we are usually in no doubt about what will happen. Even more, they absolutely love a leisurely pace, with descriptions and events drawn out in full detail. This impulse is fully evident in Book 3 of *The Odyssey*. The fact that Nestor knows nothing about Odysseus's whereabouts does not deter Homer for a single moment from recounting the entire conversation that occurred after that announcement.

As Nestor rambles on, we hear all about the end of the war at Troy, and then the homeward journeys of Nestor and Agamemnon. Homer's strategy in narrating all of this will make sense if we take a wide-angle view of "the matter of Troy" (the voluminous collection of story material dealing with the Trojan War). *The Odyssey* belongs to the category of return stories. The audience who was interested in the return of Odysseus could be trusted to be interested in the stories of other Greek heroes who returned home after the war as well. Additionally, storytellers love to work with *foils*—plot motifs or characters who set off (the literal meaning of *foil*) the main plot or character by being either a parallel or a contrast. The journey of Odysseus and his homecoming stand out all the more clearly when we set them alongside the return of heroes like Nestor, Agamemnon, and (in the next book) Menelaos.

For Reflection or Discussion

Although *The Odyssey* is a return story, as we progress through the story we keep learning more and more about the Trojan War itself; what do we learn about it in Book 3? Closely related to that, what do we learn about Odysseus as Homer pursues his technique of the delayed entrance of the hero? The main foil that is put before us is the homecomings of Agamemnon and Odysseus; where does this contrast appear in Book 3? Finally, it yields a lot to comb Book 3 for references to religious practices such as sacrifices and prayers, to the divine beings (like Athena, who accompanies Telemachos disguised as a family friend named Mentor), and to religious sentiments uttered by the human characters. Once we get beyond the crudeness of gods and goddesses being portrayed as essentially human, we can see that Homer's worldview is solidly religious (and even, as one scholar says, theological).

The Greek philosopher Aristotle (whose treatise called *The Poetics* is the oldest surviving work of literary theory that we possess) called literature an "imitation of life." Every culture likes to see its common experiences imitated in its stories. If Homer tells us in leisurely detail about arrival and leave-taking, eating and drinking in a courtly setting, journeying by boat, and the details of battle, it is because those things were part of the regular experience of the original audience.

BOOK 4
What Happened in Lacedeimon [Sparta]

Plot Summary

The next stop on the fact-finding journey of Telemachos is the palace of Menelaos in Sparta. Again the protocol of arrival and hospitality receives lavish attention. Again the conversation at court centers on the return of various Greek warriors to their homes, and again the murderous homecoming of Agamemnon is conspicuous in the account. The only information that Telemachos receives about his father is the fact that Menelaos saw him weeping on the island of Calypso, a goddess who kept Odysseus there by force.

The foregoing action occupies half of Book 4. Halfway through the book the scene suddenly shifts back to the home of Odysseus in Ithaca. We should remember that Books 1 through 4 form a

The opening description of the palace of Menelaos and the account of the protocol of hospitality that is practiced there are a picture of a domestic utopia. After the day's activities, we read that the king lay down beside Helen in her long robe; this is one of numerous snapshots in *The Odyssey* of the marriage bed as a unifying motif.

As gossipy Menelaos talks on and on at the banquet table, he voices a number of criticisms of the Trojan War. For example, he expresses the startling sentiment (right in the presence of his wife) that he wishes he had stayed at home instead of fighting the war. *The Odyssey* is an anomaly in ancient literature by elevating domestic values over the heroic (that is, warrior's) code. This epic serves as an occasion for readers to codify their own feelings and convictions about domestic values. The return to the crisis in Odysseus's kingdom with which Book 4 ends fits into this pattern as well: it shows how much has been lost because Odysseus went off to war.

Not only does *The Odyssey* elevate domestic values over military ones; it also extends that to elevate feminine values over some aspects of masculine values. (In fact, Victorian novelist Samuel Butler wrote a book entitled *The Authoress of the Odyssey* in which he argued that the author of this epic must have been a woman because it devotes so much attention to feminine values and experiences.) If we read closely, it is obvious that the

unit known as "The Telemachia" (the journey of Telemachos). We end this unit as we began it—with a vivid picture of the crisis that has engulfed the kingdom of Odysseus. After the ideal hospitality that Telemachos has received from Nestor and Menelaos, we look at the looting of Odysseus's property as the suitors devour his food and pressure Penelope to marry one of them.

Commentary

The human interest picks up in this book if we know what is happening below the surface. The wife of Menelaos is Helen. In the classical imagination, she was the most beautiful woman in the world, carried off by Paris of Troy to be his wife (and there is always a suspicion in Greek mythology that Helen went willingly). This abduction occasioned the whole Trojan War, which Menelaos and his allies conducted in order to recover Helen and bring her back to Sparta. So was this celebrity couple happily reunited? Yes and no. If we read carefully, we can see many tension points in their marriage. Helen is always needing to defend herself against suspicion of disloyalty. Menelaos actually insults Helen by saying that he wishes he had stayed at home and saved the lives lost at Troy. Our visit to the court of Menelaos thus becomes one of many passages in *The Odyssey* that criticize the warrior's code of conventional epic by showing that it destroys more than it achieves.

Several things explain the sudden shift back to Ithaca halfway through this book. One is that Homer wanted the Telemachia to have a self-contained quality as the first of three main phases to the plot. The four books devoted to the quest of Telemachos for information about his father reach closure with the return to Ithaca. Additionally, the thievery of the suitors stands out, highlighted as a contrast to the hospitality that Telemachos has been receiving during his travels. This, in turn, reaches it climax as we hear of a plot by the suitors to murder Telemachos when he returns home.

For Reflection or Discussion

The purpose of the journey of Telemachos is to receive information about his father. While the information is not as complete as Telemachos wished, he does learn something about his father. What does Telemachos learn (and we with him) about Odysseus as Book 4 unfolds (including Menelaos's story about the exploits of Odysseus at the Trojan War)? If we read closely, we find many details that undermine the heroic code that celebrated the warrior's exploits; at what points is the Trojan War itself criticized during the visit of Telemachos in the court of Menelaos? In what ways does the relationship between Menelaos and Helen stand as a contrast to that between Odysseus and Penelope?

commanding and even electrifying presence of Helen overshadows her husband, who by comparison is slow on the draw.

Menelaos ignores the primary concern of Telemachos (to learn about his father) as he long-windedly tells the story of his own travels to get home after the war. We can make sense of Homer's decision in this regard by remembering that *The Odyssey* is a return story composed for an audience who could be assumed to enjoy other return stories as well.

BOOK 5

Odysseus Leaves Calypso's Island

Plot Summary

The opening of Book 5 is a flashback to the council of the gods with which the epic began. Part of the decision reached at the council was to dispatch Hermes to the island of Calypso to order the

Archetypes abound in Book 5. The first one is Calypso's island, which is portrayed as an earthly paradise. It is a green world, lush and fertile. Why, then, doesn't it win the allegiance of Odysseus? Partly because of his loyalty to home and family, but there is more going on than this. To give in to a life of slothful ease would not satisfy the Greek and humanistic urge for action, society, and fame. To become immortal like the gods would represent oblivion to Odysseus as a human, and it would also violate his identity as the one who acts, suffers, and endures. Odysseus's encounters with deity paradoxically reinforce his proud humanity.

The heroism of Odysseus includes many specific dimensions, and the twelve adventures confront the hero with an ever-expanding list of temptations that require numerous specific virtues. It would be easy to lose sight of the overriding virtue, and we must not allow this to happen. Faithfulness to home and family is the overriding virtue and motivation displayed by Odysseus.

release of Odysseus from control of the goddess. So we accompany Hermes on his mission. Upon our arrival, the delayed entrance of the hero reaches its culmination when we finally lay eyes on Odysseus. He is conspicuously out of step with his external environment, spending every day on the shore weeping out of homesickness. The arrival of Hermes on the island occupies the first third of Book 5.

In the middle phase of Book 5 we observe Calypso follow through on the demand of the gods to release Odysseus. For seven years Calypso has held Odysseus captive, a power that she is able to exercise because she has the powers of deity. Calypso makes one last appeal to Odysseus to accept her offer (actually a temptation) to eat ambrosia and drink nectar. The significance of those two items is that they are the food and drink of the gods; if Odysseus were to partake of them, he would become immortal like the gods, and thereby cease to be human. Odysseus heroically resists the temptation.

The last third of Book 5 narrates Odysseus's preparations for his journey, the subsequent departure from the island of Calypso, and the ordeal of shipwreck at sea. After three days on the sea, Odysseus lands at a country called Phaiacia [fee-A-sha].

Commentary

There are two main characters in Book 5. One is the goddess Calypso (Greek "concealer"). She is portrayed as a "sex goddess" (an ideally attractive female), and it comes as quite a surprise that even she fits into the domestic emphasis of *The Odyssey*. Our first picture of Calypso is in a domestic setting, in front of a fireplace as she weaves on a loom. But that is a momentary picture. The chief function of Calypso is that she is the archetypal temptress. She offers Odysseus domestic comfort, feminine beauty, sex, and immortality. Odysseus rejects the temptation out of loyalty to his wife and as an assertion of his proud humanity.

The other main character is Odysseus, domestic hero *par excellence*. How, then, could he have had sexual relations with Calypso for seven years? Because he was not acting voluntarily. In the world of Greek mythology, to resist the desires of a deity would be to risk a punishment such as being turned into a tree (as Daphne was) or a prophetess whom no one heeded (as Cassandra was). The ignominy of the sexual relations between Calypso and Odysseus flows not to Odysseus but to Greek religion.

Unless we are familiar with the whole story, we have no clue as to how the seven years on Calypso's island fit into the overall story of Odysseus. The middle phase of the three-part plot of *The Odyssey* is the wanderings of Odysseus (his journey home by ship). Although the Calypso episode is the first one we encounter as we read the story, it is actually the next to last of the twelve adventures. Each of the twelve adventures can be analyzed according to a twofold grid: each one confronts Odysseus with one or more vices that must be resisted, and each one therefore requires the exercise of a virtue. In the episode of Calypso, the hero is tempted to become one of the immortal gods through indulgence of his appetites, and he exercises the virtue of abstinence from the food and drink of the gods.

The last third of Book 5 allows us to a visit a great archetype of the literary imagination—the perilous journey by sea. Psalm 107:21–32 is a good parallel passage for the story of Odysseus's seventeen-day journey, ending with arrival safely on land. The Old Testament story of Jonah (chapters 1–2) enacts the same archetype. More specifically, this is a story of shipwreck, like that endured by the apostle Paul (Acts 27) and the one portrayed in the opening scene of Shakespeare's play *The Tempest*.

The domestic theme of *The Odyssey* is embodied partly in a series of long epic similes (comparisons) that compare something in the epic to some familiar aspect of domestic life. An example occurs near the end of Book 5 when Odysseus's arrival on land after a threat to his life is compared to the welcome with which a family greets the healing of the father after a long illness.

For Reflection or Discussion

Epic is a branch of hero story. Since Book 5 is our first direct encounter with the hero (after numerous references to him), it is a particularly good episode with which to ponder what is heroic about Odysseus. Second, since virtually everything in *The Odyssey* elevates domestic values, we can analyze the details that fit into the glorification of the domestic. Third, a temptation story needs to make the temptation alluring; what details make Calypso's island attractive on the surface?

BOOK 6

How Odysseus Appealed to Nausicaa, and How She Brought Him to Her Father's House

Plot Summary

At the end of Book 5 we observed Odysseus landing on the coast of a country called Phaiacia. Book 6 narrates a domestic scene that takes place in the palace of King Alcinoos prior to Odysseus's arrival there. Homer invents a scene to achieve the purpose of having the king's daughter Nausicaa on the seacoast to help rescue Odysseus. He invents an episode in which Nausicaa has a dream of wanting to be married. Upon awakening, Nausicaa asks her father for permission to wash her clothes in the river adjacent to the coast where Odysseus has landed. With that bit of explanation in place, the main event of Book 6 is ready to occur.

As Nausicaa and her friends are playing games after washing their clothes, Odysseus steps out of a thicket. He appeals to the young girl to help him survive. The formal exchange between Odysseus and Nausicaa is a high point of rhetoric in *The Odyssey*. The upshot is that Nausicaa gives Odysseus instructions regarding how to enter her parents' palace and appeal to them for help. The function of Book 6 is thus a preparation for an action to follow.

Commentary

Odysseus's visit to Phaiacia is the last of his twelve adventures (though the second about which we read). The key to Book 6 is the characterization of Nausicaa and what she represents. Considered in herself, she is youthful femininity in its most idealized form. In contrast to the immortal goddess Calypso, Nausicaa is thoroughly human and at a transition point in her life between girlhood and womanhood. Exactly what does Homer intend with a whole book devoted to this winsome young woman?

The key to answering that is to be alert that every one of the twelve adventures of Odysseus is a temptation of some sort. This adventure (which extends into subsequent books after being introduced here) is so subtle that we could miss it. There were multiple ways of getting Nausicaa to the seacoast, but Homer makes the goddess Athena enter the palace and say to Nausicaa in a dream that it is time for her to marry. In other words, a romantic love motif is clearly introduced into the story.

That motif is kept alive. When Odysseus first speaks to Nausicaa, he includes the statement that the person who marries Nausicaa will be blessed beyond measure, and he ends that same speech with a wish that Nausicaa will be happily married. Later Nausicaa expresses the innocent wish to her companions that she might have someone like Odysseus for a husband. What is going on? As

Not only do literary *authors* show that they have a worldview; so do literary critics and classroom teachers of literature. Literary commentary on a text such as Book 6 of *The Odyssey* shows a range of ethical viewpoints, and it is important for readers not to be swept into assenting to something that is contrary to their own convictions. One literary critic acknowledges that Homer did not allow Odysseus's encounter with Nausicaa to escalate into a romantic relationship, but this same critic laments this fact, adding that the happiest ending imaginable for *The Odyssey* would be for Odysseus to marry Nausicaa and stay in Phaiacia. All of this is to say that Christian readers must be as discerning of literary critics as they are of literary authors.

The dialogue between Odysseus and Nausicaa in the middle of Book 6 is a model of formal rhetoric. Its function is to (a) elevate the dignity of this famous encounter between two strangers, and (b) do justice to the delicacy of the situation. There is also a latent persuasive element (hinted in the text by the statement that Odysseus "spoke to her in gentle and persuasive words"): Odysseus looks absolutely awful (and is naked, besides) after his shipwreck at sea, and yet he needs to persuade a young girl to help him gain admittance to the palace of her parents.

The elevation of women in *The Odyssey* is universally acknowledged. A small example of it occurs near the end of Book 6 when Nausicaa instructs Odysseus regarding what he must do when he enters the palace of her parents. The whole focus is on Nausicaa's mother, not her father, and Odysseus is instructed to go right up to her mother, giving the impression that it is her opinion that will count most.

the time that Odysseus spends in Phaiacia continues to unfold, temptation of the subtlest kind is encountered and mastered by Odysseus. It is the temptation for Odysseus to fall in love with Nausicaa, settle down in what turns out to be a domestic utopia, and forget about home and wife.

For Reflection or Discussion

Two plotlines unfold in Book 6. The foreground action is that Odysseus needs to be rescued from his dangerous situation. We can relish the skill with which Homer conducts the stylized dialogue between Odysseus and Nausicaa as they move toward a game plan for maneuvering Odysseus into a position to appeal for help to the king and queen of the realm. The rhetoric of the dialogue can be analyzed as the epitome of delicacy and decorum. The second, subsurface plotline is the temptation motif. Nausicaa does not set out to seduce Odysseus; she is a frank and naive young woman with innocent intentions. Similarly, Odysseus is focused on being rescued, not in courting a young woman. Nonetheless, we should notice two things in regard to this: (1) the string of references to marriage; (2) the qualities of Nausicaa that would make her an appealing young woman to marry.

BOOK 7

What Happened to Odysseus in the Palace of Alcinoos

Plot Summary

Book 6 laid the groundwork for Odysseus to enter town and be rescued by the king and queen; Book 7 is the sequel in which we see the game plan executed. As Odysseus enters the city hidden by a mist, Athena shows up and repeats the instructions that Nausicaa had given Odysseus in the preceding book. After a crescendo of increasing expectancy, we finally reach the climax as Odysseus stands before the glittering palace of Alcinoos and Arete. Then Odysseus, still concealed in a mist, enters the hall in a moment of high drama.

In keeping with the domestic theme of *The Odyssey*, the protocol of receiving a stranger comes to dominate the action in the second half of Book 7. In effect, we as readers have arrived in Phaiacia with Odysseus, and we, too, gradually learn about the place. More importantly, King Alcinoos asks two very legitimate questions of Odysseus: who are you? and where do you come from? Odysseus replies by recounting only the seven-year stay on Calypso's island, along with his shipwreck after that (instigated by the god Poseidon, and we later learn why).

Commentary

Phaiacia will gradually emerge in our imagination as a utopia—the archetypal "good place." For example, it is a remote place exempt from the vices of civilization. The gods visit the city without dis-

The "good place" motif that we encounter as we read the descriptions of the palace of Phaiacia is an impulse that underlies much literature. One of the functions of literature is to codify what people want in life. The splendor of the palace and its orchard can be explored for the ideals they embody—wealth, for example, and beauty, and abundance, and a well-ordered household. We can note as well that this picture elevates domestic values, something that this epic never ceases to do.

We need to guard against dismissing the references to the gods and goddesses simply because they seem less than divine to Christian sensibilities. After the description of the palace and its orchard, the narrator adds the sentiment that these were the glorious gifts that gods had granted to Alcinoos. Almost immediately after that, in one of many domestic beatitudes scattered throughout *The Odyssey*, Odysseus includes the wish that the gods might grant the assembled people to be happy and have children to inherit their wealth. Homer the pagan poet is expressing what Christians believe about divine providence. Perhaps we can think of Homer as receiving some of the "good dreams" that C. S. Lewis says God sent to the ancient pagans.

Storytellers love to work with heightened contrasts (the technique known as "foil"). Throughout Book 7 Homer manages the descriptions in such a way as to heighten the contrast between the prosperity of Alcinoos and the deprivation of Odysseus. In the hall, for example, we read, "There they were, face to face, the King in his majesty, and the castaway with only his knowledge of man and his ready wit." At the very end of the book, we read that Odysseus slept after all his troubles, but [contrast] Alcinoos lay beside his wife.

guise. And so forth. Within this idealized setting, the palace itself is resplendent—the best of the best. In fact, as Odysseus is before the palace, we get two extended descriptions that are a famous "set piece" of description in Greek literature. One passage describes "the great mansion" (that is, the building), and a balancing passage describes the orchard at the palace.

When Odysseus recounts what happened to him most recently during his ten-year journey, he is actually warming up for what will occupy the next five books of the epic, which are devoted to the hero's account of his wanderings. But it is a foreshadowing only, as Homer reins in Odysseus's account of his journey and returns to the reception of Odysseus at the palace. As the household winds down for the night, Odysseus "slept after all his troubles."

For Reflection or Discussion

Three avenues of analysis will yield what Book 7 has to offer. One is to trace the references that make Phaiacia a utopia. As part of this motif, we should note additionally the ways in which the wanderer Odysseus stands in stark contrast to the idealized nature of the place he is visiting. Second, we should continue to notice how Homer weaves variations on his domestic theme throughout the story in big and small ways. To cite just one example, the concluding picture in Book 7 is the marriage bed—king and queen lying beside each other for the night. Third, the latent temptation represented by Nausicaa surfaces late in the book when King Alcinoos suddenly offers the opinion that it would be wonderful if Odysseus stayed and married his daughter.

BOOK 8

How They Held Games and Sports in Phaiacia

Plot Summary

Almost everything that an epic storyteller incorporates into his story is drawn from the storehouse of epic conventions. Since Homer's epics are the fountainhead of Western epic, we always need to entertain the possibility that Homer started a given convention. The main action of Book 8—games and entertainment on a grand scale—is an epic convention. In *The Odyssey*, the games are an interlude—a lull in the intensity of Odysseus's ordeals. As Book 8 unfolds, we are introduced to a full range of recreations in the ancient world, from the performance of an epic to physical sports like running and wrestling. Odysseus competes in the physical contests, allowing him to display his prowess while among friends.

Half of Book 8 is devoted to the storytelling of the epic poet as he entertains the assembled audience (showing how prominent epic was in ancient cultures). No fewer than three pages are devoted to a summary of the epic that was performed in Phaiacia as part of the entertainment at the banquet held in honor of Odysseus.

Halfway through Book 8 the motif of games and sports is dropped, and the focus shifts to interaction between the host city and its visitor. We observe the rituals of hospitality, including the giving of gifts to Odysseus. Odysseus and Nausicaa have their final exchange as they are both going into the banquet hall. The dinner hour entertainment consists of the epic storyteller recounting the events

Since we are reading and interpreting an epic, it is of special interest to see how epic storytelling was regarded in the very culture that produced *The Odyssey*. Book 8 elevates epic to the status of "the best of the best" in the category of entertainment. Epic is called "a divine gift." When the blind minstrel arrives in the hall to perform, he becomes the center of attention. Odysseus wants the marshal to give the storyteller his kindest regards, adding that "in every nation of mankind upon the earth minstrels have honor and respect." We might note that the portrait of this particular epic storyteller as blind has been interpreted through the ages as Homer's self-portrait, since legend holds that Homer was blind.

One of the Phaiacians, named Broadsea, insults Odysseus by saying that he doesn't have the look of an athlete. The insult serves at least two purposes. It is a foil to the hospitable behavior of the other Phaiacians toward their guest. It also prompts Odysseus to assert himself and show his prowess while among friends. In fact, Odysseus utters a brief boast of his military exploits, entirely in keeping with the heroic code that prevails in the epic tradition as a whole.

"All I want is to get home," says Odysseus to excuse not having his mind on the games. "May the gods grant you to come safe to your native land, and see your wife," says Broadsea when he makes up for his insult to Odysseus. *The Odyssey* is saturated with small touches that accentuate the primacy that this epic assigns to home, family, and domestic values. As we read, we need to be receptive to the cumulative weight of these references.

In a poignant moment, the storyteller pictures Nausicaa as looking her best—"as lovely as if she had stepped down from heaven" and gazing with admiring eyes at Odysseus. She expresses a courteous wish for Odysseus to have a happy voyage, and Odysseus replies with a decorous statement of gratitude to Nausicaa for saving his life. This is the end of the encounter between the eminently marriageable young woman and the hero. Homer has managed the moment with delicacy, in obvious contrast

of the Trojan War, including exploits of Odysseus himself. Odysseus weeps as he listens, and the king responds by inquiring who Odysseus is.

Commentary

On one level, an entire book in *The Odyssey* given to sports and entertainment strikes a festive and celebrative note. If epic exists to sum up what a whole age wants to say, then obviously the importance of recreation and leisure are a legitimate inclusion. They are part of the good life as virtually all civilizations have envisioned it. But as is always the case in *The Odyssey*, there are subtle subcurrents below the surface action.

As *The Odyssey* continues to unfold, it becomes an increasingly strong critique of the warrior's code that is usually celebrated in ancient epic. That critique surfaces strongly in Book 8. Early and late in the book we observe Odysseus's response to the epic performer's account of events at the Trojan War where Odysseus had fought. We would expect Odysseus to respond favorably to the story of his exploits, but instead he weeps. At this point we are left to speculate as to why Odysseus is so troubled by the spectacle of military conflict, but at least a strong note of disapproval has been sounded in regard to the martial theme that is overwhelmingly glorified in conventional epic.

Even further below the surface is the latent temptation of romantic love represented by Nausicaa. Homer terminates the relationship between Nausicaa and Odysseus without allowing it to become a full-fledged romance, in keeping with his ideal of married love as permanent and faithful. A critic comments that "temptation of the subtlest sort has been met and mastered." The virtues that the hero displays are self-control, discretion, and a sense of propriety.

For Reflection or Discussion

Literature exists partly to give us images of the good life. Homer gives us such images to ponder and celebrate. More specifically, we can analyze what Homer and his age regarded as enlightened recreation and leisure, and then consider how our own ideal compares to it. Second, Homer loves to keep his domestic theme alive in our imaginations with passing references to motifs that stretch throughout his epic. For example, characters in the story again and again express good wishes that have a domestic focus. Thus midway through Book 8, as the action shifts from competitive sports to the oral performance of an epic, Alcinoos expresses the sentiment to Odysseus that when he is "at home again and sitting at dinner in [his] hall with [his] wife and children," he will remember with pleasure the games that occurred in Phaiacia. How many other instances of the domestic theme are sprinkled throughout Book 8? Finally, we need to ferret out the small suggestions that *The Odyssey* is critical of the warrior's code. At what moments does Homer introduce details that criticize warfare?

to how most modern storytellers would handle the matter.

In addition to the myriad domestic blessings and wishes expressed by characters in *The Odyssey*, there is a string of epic similes that keep domestic values before us. One of these comes near the end of Book 8, where Odysseus's weeping is compared to the weeping of a wife whose husband falls in battle. The cruel fate of the widow of war is described so vividly that we can recognize this as the most severe indictment yet of the warrior's code. What the warfare destroys is domestic values. Odysseus's pride at his accomplishments is suddenly transformed into pity for his victims.

BOOK 9

How Odysseus Visited the Lotus-Eaters and the Cyclops

Plot Summary

At the very beginning of the book Odysseus gives us one of the best descriptions we have of what an oral

The hit-and-run raid that Odysseus's men conduct against the Ciconians is par for the course according to the warrior's code. But instead of being commended, the action of Odysseus's men is what brings threat and destruction to the crew. Zeus, the chief deity in the world of the story, sends a storm on the travelers in punishment for what they did. The men give in to greed and self-indulgence (when they lounge on the beach instead of taking off), and the virtues that were required (and here violated) were self-control and respect for the lives and property of others. Proverbs 1:10–19 provides good commentary on the episode.

The only thing that the episode of the lotus-eaters shares with the preceding episode is that it is brief. It involves a plant rather than people, and it is mild rather than violent. At one level, eating the lotus plant represents a temptation to sloth, indolence, and indulgence of the appetites. The virtue required is abstinence. But there is more than this. The lotus plant induces forgetfulness, and for this particular crew forgetfulness of home. The overriding virtue required of Odysseus and his crew is faithfulness to home. Within such a framework, this is one of Homer's nightmare passages, even though we might like the prospect of lounging on the beach.

performance of epic was like in ancient cultures. Then Odysseus answers the question that Alcinoos had asked him near the end of Book 8, namely, what his name is. That is a transition to Odysseus's account of his ten years of wandering after he left Troy. This is the flashback that every epic contains. Epics begin "in the middle of things," at a point of great crisis. Halfway through the story the author devises a narrative situation that takes us back to the actual beginning of the story (as distinct from the plot, which is the arrangement of the story to fit the author's overall design).

The Odyssey narrates what happens during the ten years after the Trojan War (which in turn took ten years to fight). What happened chiefly was a series of twelve ordeals or adventures that Odysseus endured on his journey home. We already know about the last two stops on the journey—Calypso's island and Phaiacia. In the cozy surroundings of a banquet held in his honor, Odysseus becomes the storyteller for the first ten adventures. Book 9 narrates three memorable events on Odysseus's perilous journey: a violent people called the Ciconians, drug-consuming beach people, and a one-eyed monster who eats men for breakfast.

Commentary

For modern readers, the adventures of Odysseus are the most memorable part of *The Odyssey*, and with the right analytic grid we can explain why. We encounter the pleasures of the adventure story in their pure form. Adventure stories specialize in extraordinary events. Variety of action is a staple in such stories, and settings are often remote and exotic. Conflict and danger are heightened, and spectacular feats are a regular feature. Surprises abound. Common ingredients include storms, disguises, shipwrecks, battles, journeys through dangerous landscapes, chases, hiding, arrests, and escapes. In order to relish such a story, we need to summon a childlike response.

In the middle books of *The Odyssey*, the conventions of the adventure story merge with those of fantasy. Fantasy is at the opposite end of the literary continuum from realism. It does not reproduce the world around us but whisks us away to an alternate world—a strange world. Supernatural characters and events are the norm in a fantasy story. English Romantic poet Samuel Taylor Coleridge theorized that we need to *suspend our disbelief* when we read fantasy stories.

But we should not read Homer's engaging story only as a child does. The key to seeing the deeper meanings of Homer's adventure story is to realize that the fantastic details are *metaphors of the human condition*. They are not factually true, but they are true to human experience at the level of issues presented. We need to *bridge the gap* between the fantastic details in the story and our own experiences. To prime the pump in this regard, here is a beginning list of what Odysseus encounters in his wanderings: violence, threat to life, forbidden sex, encounters with women, drugs, the occult, lost luggage and passport, eating, the hostility of the elements (especially the sea), forbidden food and drink, homesickness, getting lost, culture shock, hospitality and its opposite, and inadequate transportation. For all their far-flung fantasy, the wanderings of Odysseus are as recognizable as the journeys that we or our friends have taken, and Odysseus himself emerges as the archetypal tourist.

When we come to the episode of the Cyclops, the principle "now for something completely different" kicks in. It is a long, long episode. The agent is a supernatural monster (a giant, no less), and the episode is violent in the extreme. It is one of Homer's most interesting compositions. Two things tempt Odysseus to stay in the cave when he should have moved on: what Odysseus sees in the cave excites his curiosity, and in addition he is greedy in wanting to claim the visitor's gift. Odysseus should have exercised the virtue of self-restraint. Once he is trapped in the cave, Odysseus displays wit, intelligence, and cleverness.

Homer's favorite epithet for his hero is "clever Odysseus." Odysseus displays his cleverness in this episode in the following ways: he says that his name is "no man" (so when the Cyclops yells when his eye is gouged out and says to his neighbors that "no man" is killing him, his neighbors ignore his pleas); he makes the monster drunk so he can gouge out his eye; he tells the Cyclops that his ship was wrecked (whereas it was actually out in the harbor where the Cyclops could have smashed it); he ties himself and his men on the underside of the sheep so as to escape detection when escaping from the cave.

This episode, too, undercuts the warrior's code. When as a parting gesture Odysseus shouts out his name to the Cyclops, he is uttering the standard warrior's boast. But that very boast allows the Cyclops to pray to his father, the god Poseidon, god of the sea, to avenge his loss of his eye. Poseidon responds by making Odysseus's journey a continuous narrow escape on the sea.

In this epic Homer never misses an opportunity to flaunt his praise of domestic values. The opening of Book 10 paints a brief picture of the ideal family; in fact, the floating island of Aiolia is a domestic utopia. When Odysseus returns to the island after the men have unleashed the winds from the bag, Aiolos is "feasting with his wife and children." When Aiolos tells Odysseus

For Reflection or Discussion

The following grid will yield big dividends as we analyze the individual adventures of Odysseus. First, variety of adventure is a particular virtue of Homer's technique. As we keep progressing through the adventures, Homer changes *the length of the episodes* (e.g., brief for the Ciconians and lotus eaters, long for the Cyclops); *the mildness or violence of the event*; and *the nature of the agents* involved (e.g., humans for the Ciconians, a plant for the island of the lotus eaters, a monster in the Cyclops episode). Additionally, each one of the adventures is a *temptation* to one or more vices, and each requires the exercise of one or more *virtues* before Odysseus can escape the threat. How does each of the adventures narrated in Book 9 line up in regard to these considerations? Additionally, it is important to keep compiling a list of ways in which *The Odyssey* undercuts the heroic code that glorified warfare and the taking of spoils from the battlefield.

BOOK 10

The Island of the Winds; the Land of the Midnight Sun; Circe

Plot Summary

In Book 10 Homer keeps up his rhythm of three adventures per book (more specifically, two short episodes followed by a long one). He also stays the course in regard to providing variety of adventure, and he makes the individual episodes tests or temptations that require the display of an appropriate virtue. The floating island of the winds (the island is named Aiolia) is a domestic utopia. What could possibly go wrong here? After leaving the island, Odysseus and his men sail for ten days and are actually in sight of Ithaca, when Odysseus relaxes his guard and falls asleep. His men open the bag of winds to satisfy their curiosity and greed, and the ship promptly arrives back at the island of Aiolia.

The visit to the land of the Lystrygonians is the opposite of the previous adventure (except that it, too, is narrated briefly). Instead of the mildness of a floating island, Odysseus's men receive a murderous reception. Only the ship of Odysseus escapes (as clever Odysseus had tied his ship outside the harbor). Then comes an episode to rival the stay on Calypso's island—one that occurs on the island of the goddess Circe. Circe is an enchantress with the power to transform men into animals. Only by following the instructions of the god Hermes and using a charm in addition is Odysseus able to resist Circe and compel her to transform Odysseus's men back into humans. It is another nightmare passage. As Odysseus makes preparation to leave the enchanted island, Circe informs him that he must next visit Hades, the abode of the dead (the realm of the afterlife). Odysseus and his men are terrified by the prospect.

Commentary

A good avenue toward appreciating Homer's accomplishment in this part of his epic is to look for evidences of his skill with the genre of the adventure story. The range of types of episodes (long/short, violent/mild, human/supernatural agents) shows Homer's inventiveness. Additionally, we can

to get off his island at once and calls him and his men an enemy of the gods, we can see (says one commentator) the Greek bias against a loser.

A particular virtue of the travel story genre is that it allows for inventiveness in imagining remote and strange places. The massacre at the country of the Lystrygonians gets hardly more than a page, but the episode wins us with the evocative picture of a place of continuous sunlight, and also with the vividness with which the massacre of Odysseus's men is described.

C. S. Lewis once wrote a classic (short!) essay entitled "On Stories." It is obvious that Lewis greatly prized the element of atmosphere in stories, and he singles out the Circe episode in *The Odyssey* for favorable comment: "It is here that Homer shows his supreme excellence. The landing on Circe's island, the sight of smoke going up from amidst those unexplored woods, the god meeting us . . . what an anti-climax if all these had been the prelude only to some ordinary risk of life and limb! But the peril that lurks here . . . is worthy of the setting."

There is also symbolism at work in the Circe episode. Before Circe waves her magic wand to transform men into animals, she puts a drug into their food that makes them forget their homeland. The symbolism: to forget home is to lose one's humanity and in fact to become less than human.

The men's response to the news that they must visit the abode of the dead is as effective a foreshadowing as can be imagined. Odysseus sits on his bed and no longer cares to live. His men groan and tear out their hair. Homer also inserts a note of symbolism into this sensational action. Elpenor, youngest companion on the voyage, loses his composure and unthinkingly jumps from the roof where he has been sleeping. This loss of life is a substitute for Odysseus, who is allowed to enter the abode of the dead and return to life (Virgil would later imitate the scene in his epic *The Aeneid*).

admire the variety of (a) sins to which Odysseus and his men are tempted and (b) the virtues that are required (either to prevent catastrophe or to escape once catastrophe has occurred).

A sense of life begins to emerge from the story of Odysseus's wanderings, and we need to analyze and name the ingredients of that outlook (which is both a worldview and an ethic or code of moral behavior). Obviously Homer views life as a continuous test for people, who must choose between virtue and vice, wisdom and folly. In Homer's story, the greatest and omnipresent danger is to forget home, as Odysseus obviously does during an indulgent, year-long stay on Circe's island (though we need to note that Odysseus learned a lesson from it, as witnessed by his later behavior on Calypso's island). Correspondingly, the prime virtue is faithfulness to home and family.

The general tenor of the temptations is that they represent some form of indulgence of feelings or appetites. Self-control and denial of the appetites thus emerge as an important part of Homer's ethical outlook. Having noted Homer's worldview and ethos, we can start thinking of biblical examples and passages that embody a similar viewpoint.

For Reflection or Discussion

The commentary stated above about the sense of life that emerges from Book 10 is a beginning only. Further probing of this subject will yield a lot. At the level of the story as a story, the inventiveness of Homer's imagination can be analyzed. Novelist Thomas Hardy claimed that "a story must be exceptional enough to justify its telling." Simply asking what sparks interest in a given episode or passage can be a springboard to good analysis and insight.

BOOK 11

How Odysseus Visited the Kingdom of the Dead

Plot Summary

Here Homer varies his pattern of multiple episodes per book, concentrating everything on the visit to the underworld (which became an established epic convention). This expansive episode breaks down into six distinct units, with an unexpected interlude interjected into the middle of the book, so the book seems even more packed than the three-episode books that have preceded.

The build-up to the journey to Hades at the end of the preceding book had been intense, leading us to expect a horror story. Homer does not disappoint us when we come to the actual journey. The entrance to the underworld is shrouded in darkness. Awe-inspiring sacrifices are performed, and then a crowd of souls of the dead gather around, making Odysseus pale with fear. This is our tip-off that the thing to which Odysseus and his men are tempted in this episode is fear. The virtue required is courage.

The format that Homer decided upon was a series of six encounters between Odysseus and selected shades of the dead. The first interview is with Elpenor, who had died when leaping from the roof (as narrated at the end of the preceding book); Elpenor requests that he be properly mourned and buried. Then Teiresias, the blind prophet of Greek mythology, steps forward and dispenses a few instructions to Odysseus regarding the rest of his journey home. Third, Odysseus inquires about his family's situation from his mother (about whose

The entrance to the underworld is a literary example of the numinous—the supernatural and holy. Homer does a masterful job of evoking the mystery of the place and of distancing it from ordinary reality. The sacrifices that Odysseus performs heighten the effect. Any reader familiar with Dante's *Inferno* can see that Dante got his basic strategy for a mortal's journey through the afterlife from Homer, including the format of recording the traveler's responses to the places and people he meets in the afterlife.

The ostensible purpose of the journey to Hades is to receive instruction for the rest of the journey. This instructive mission is transacted in the dialogue with the blind prophet Teiresias. Among the important things in the speech of Teiresias are these: affirmation of the worth of home; a warning about the hostility of Poseidon against Odysseus on his journey; assurance that Odysseus will reach home after many sufferings; the need for Odysseus and his men to control themselves in the face of temptations.

The dialogue between Odysseus and his mother is not only filled with emotion and human interest; it also reinforces the domestic emphasis of the epic as a whole. The threefold, futile attempt of Odysseus to embrace the ghost of his mother became a familiar motif in later literature.

Literary critics commonly regard the three encounters with fallen warriors as being among Homer's most inspired creations. If we look at the exchanges between Odysseus and the fallen heroes carefully, we can see that they undercut the heroic code (the glorification of warfare and conquest). Agamemnon went off the fight at Troy only to come home to a faithless wife and his own murder. When Odysseus attempts to console Achilles by informing him how honored he is in the world, Achilles immediately cuts him off and laments his status as a famous but fallen warrior. The continuing despair of Ajax (who chooses silence as the most effective way of expressing his resentment) over losing the arms of Achilles to Odysseus leads Odysseus to remark that he wishes he had never won the trophy.

death Odysseus now learns for the first time). Fourth, we are given a long catalog of famous heroines from Greek mythology (and we might note that catalogs or lists are an expected part of epic style).

Then, without transition or explanation, Odysseus's story of his journey to the underworld is interrupted by a return to the setting where Odysseus is telling the story of his adventures, namely, the banquet hall of the palace in Phaiacia. As King Alcinoos compliments Odysseus on his storytelling ability, he draws attention to features of *The Odyssey* itself, namely, that it shows the artist's finish, that the storyteller understands his craft, and that the story of Odysseus's travels is a tale of marvels (in tribute to the fantasy element in this part of *The Odyssey*).

Still more memorable events await us as we finish the journey through the underworld. One of them is itself broken into three separate encounters with ghosts of warriors who died at the Trojan War: Agamemnon, who cannot get over the murderous treachery of his wife; Achilles, who bemoans his life in Hades but is consoled when Odysseus tells him about his son's triumphs in the war; and Ajax, who had committed suicide when Odysseus rather than he received the armor of Achilles when he died in battle.

The sixth unit in the trip through Hades is a spectacle of Minos, judge of the underworld, pronouncing judgment on the dead as they arrive. The resulting passage is a catalog of male figures from Greek mythology to match the earlier catalog of heroines. To underscore that fear is the obstacle that Odysseus needs to conquer in this episode, we end the book as we began it—with Odysseus's acknowledgment that he "grew pale with fear."

Commentary

An initial explanation for this book is that epics are expansive in nature and that this requires the storyteller to include a complete cosmology (picture of the universe) in his epic. Cosmology, in turn, requires a conception of the unseen spiritual world, including the afterlife. While Homer does as well as his worldview allows in this regard, by New Testament standards the eschatology in Book 11 is decidedly hazy. The afterlife, for Homer, is a shadowy lifelessness that replaces all that the Greek spirit most valued—action, vigor, achievement, fame.

The encounters between Odysseus and various ghosts in the underworld are dialogues or interviews. A wealth of human interest resides in each one. We should be alert, too, to the range of roles that emerges for Odysseus as epic hero. For example, he is leader of a crew dealing with the death of a crewmember. He is captain of a voyage receiving instructions for the rest of his journey. He is a family man asking his mother to fill him in on news of the family. He is a guest of the king and queen in Phaiacia. He is a warrior interacting with fellow warriors.

Death for Homer, writes a critic, "is the loss of all vital powers, a shadowy impotence that replaces vigor, action, personality, and sunshine." Here are some Bible passages that contrast that with the living hope of Christian eschatology: Job 19:25–27; Dan. 12:3; 1 Cor. 15:35–58; Heb. 12:22–24; 1 Pet. 1:3–9; Revelation 21. Homer's pictures of the afterlife make us dread it; the effect of the biblical pictures is to make us feel that we can hardly wait to get there.

For Reflection or Discussion

We need to assimilate Homer's picture of the underworld (afterlife) with our own eschatological beliefs in mind. Book 11 is the classical world's attempt at eschatology; we need to measure its inadequacy and the unsatisfying feelings that it leaves by the standard of New Testament eschatological passages. Positively, we can admire Book 11 as a high point of Homer's achievement in *The Odyssey*. As hinted in the commentary section above, the interviews between Odysseus and various ghosts are replete with human interest, and we need to take the time to probe the human and relational dynamics at work in each interview. As we do so, we should keep our antennae up for further evidences that *The Odyssey* is a domestic epic that elevates home and family and denigrates warfare and the warrior's code.

BOOK 12

The Singing Sirens, the Terrors of Scylla and Charybdis, and the Cattle of Helios

Plot Summary

With Book 12 we return to the three-episode format (and again we have two short episodes followed by a long one). The action begins with a note of surprise—a return trip to Circe to conduct the promised burial of Elpenor. In another surprise, Circe tells Odysseus what will happen in his final three adventures, so that as readers we experience those events twice. The first stop is on the island of the famous Sirens—bewitching goddesses who lure men to their island with their singing and then devour them. The episode is handled briefly, and Odysseus escapes the allurement only because he has plugged his sailors' ears with wax so they cannot hear the song of the Sirens.

Scylla and Charybdis, also supernatural females, are likewise treated summarily by Homer. They are rocky cliffs between which the ship of Odysseus must pass. In another nightmare pas-

Circe's preview of the next three adventures reminds us that epic storytellers prefer foreshadowing to suspense as a plot strategy. Additionally, Circe's account gives us as readers some helpful information by which to understand all that is happening when Odysseus undergoes the next three tests.

sage, Odysseus unavoidably loses six of his men. Knowing that he cannot escape without losing men, Odysseus is tempted to fear and cowardice, and he displays courage in going forward.

The episode that receives extended treatment is the island of the sun god Helios. Circe had warned Odysseus that the crew must avoid killing the cattle of Helios if they hoped to pass safely. Odysseus was unable to prevent his men from landing on the island, and their stay becomes a test because lack of wind keeps the men on the island for a month. The men kill some of the cattle of Helios for food, and Zeus punishes them for what the epic narrator had called folly in his opening invocation by striking their ship with a storm. Only Odysseus survives, and he lands on the island of Calypso. With that announcement the flashback in the middle of *The Odyssey* is complete.

Commentary

As we reach closure on the middle section of Homer's story—the wanderings of Odysseus—it is obvious that one of the virtues of this part of the story is the genre of the travel story to which it belongs. It is no wonder that storytellers from time immemorial have gravitated to the journey motif for their story material. The virtues of the travel story are obvious—variety of adventure and locale, danger, suspense, testing, encounters with unknown characters and customs, encounter with the divine. Movement provides impetus for the plot. Something new and exciting is always happening. The framework of the travel story can help codify events not only in Book 12 but also in the preceding books.

To tell a story is (a) to entertain and (b) to make a statement. Balancing the narrative excite-

The wanderings of Odysseus, and other parts of *The Odyssey* as well, are the very epitome of fantasy literature. This makes it all the more surprising that from time immemorial scholars and laypeople alike have been certain that the places in Homer's story, and even some of the people, are rooted in real life. In fact, numerous people and groups have attempted to retrace the journey of Odysseus in the Mediterranean region. One example among many that Homer is working with real-life details is the pair of monsters that we know as Scylla and Charybdis. As figures of the mythological imagination, they are purely imaginary, but the description that Homer gives suggests that his imagination was working with real-life materials, namely, a place called the Strait of Messina. In turn, it is a tribute to the power of the imagination that when people in real life face a difficult choice between two incompatible possibilities, we refer to the person as being between Scylla and Charybdis.

As we wind down the wanderings of Odysseus, we can note two motifs that have been prominent. One is the sea. The most persistent threat to Odysseus is water, and we note in turn that Poseidon, god of the sea, has made the sea voyage of Odysseus treacherous because Odysseus gouged out the eye of his son Polyphemos (the Cyclops). Related to this prominence of the sea, seven of the twelve adventures involve islands. Secondly, we can scarcely be unaware of how prominent females are in the wanderings of Odysseus. Not only do they often dominate the events and men; they are usually a threat to men.

ment provided by Homer's travel story is our awareness that he intends to embody a sense of life for his readers' edification. In Book 12, we are again reminded that Homer regards life as a test that requires people to choose between virtue and vice. Additionally, by choosing to end the story of Odysseus's wanderings with an incident involving the god Helios and punishment by the chief deity Zeus, Homer makes it impossible for us to ignore his religious orientation.

For Reflection or Discussion

As we reach closure on the wanderings of Odysseus, it is natural to take stock of Books 5–12 as a whole. What makes this story so famous that translator W. H. D. Rouse can call it "the best story ever written"? What is Homer best at as a storyteller? What are your favorite episodes and/ or general qualities of the narrative of the wanderings of Odysseus? If we then move from the story qualities to the question of theme, what wisdom and illumination does Homer offer us as we ponder the deeper meanings of what he says about life by means of his exciting adventure story? The fact that the *theology* of Homer is impossible should not obscure the ways in which his *morality* is often congruent with Christian morality.

BOOK 13

How Odysseus Came to Ithaca

Plot Summary

The first piece of narrative business that this book transacts is the leave-taking of Odysseus from

Phaiacia. When the gift-giving is completed, the Phaiacians transport Odysseus to his homeland, the island of Ithaca. To heighten the sense of transition between the wanderings and homecoming of Odysseus, Homer portrays Odysseus as sleeping through the voyage and awaking when he reaches Ithaca. And to keep the element of conflict alive, Homer invents a scene in which Poseidon, seeing that he can no longer thwart Odysseus, transforms the Phaiacian ship into stone as it enters the harbor, also encircling the city with a ring of mountains. The two phases of action are thus decisively separated.

With Odysseus safely deposited, his "patron goddess" Athena joins him. Athena has been largely absent from the wanderings of Odysseus, an index to Greek humanism with its ideal of self-reliance. With Athena present "to make plans for you" (as she tells Odysseus), we are given a preview of what will happen in the third phase of the plot. Athena assures Odysseus that he will conquer the suitors. More important than that is her instruction that Odysseus must tell no one that he has returned, and to complete the sense of secrecy Athena disguises Odysseus as a beggar and vagabond. In other words, the homecoming of Odysseus will be one of the most sustained performances of dramatic irony in Western literature (based on the fact that we as readers know something that characters in the story do not).

Commentary

The first thing we need to do is take stock of the overall proportions of *The Odyssey*. The wanderings of Odysseus are such a memorable story that

After the exotic flavor of Odysseus's wanderings in fantasyland, Homer sounds a series of domestically oriented notes at the beginning of Book 13. The gift giving that the Phaiacians shower on their guest as he leaves belongs to the code of hospitality, which is an expression of domestic values. Then we get an epic simile that draws upon domestic life—a man longing for supper at the end of a working day. Odysseus pronounces a domestic prayer or benediction on himself and the Phaiacians. His very last words in Phaiacia are another domestic benediction: "A blessing on you in this house, and your children."

As we listen to the instructions that Athena gives to Odysseus, it is easy to see that dramatic irony will be a mainspring of the plot in the homecoming phase of the story. We should not overlook the corresponding test motif. Odysseus's ability to maintain his disguise and control his emotions when he is mistreated will be tested, but actually *everyone* in Ithaca will have his or her loyalty or disloyalty to Odysseus tested as well.

we might make the mistake of thinking that the great things are now over. But Homer devotes the entire second half of his epic to the actual homecoming, showing that he regarded it as the consummation of his story. We need to read the second half through that lens.

The function of Book 13 is to provide a preparation for what follows. Just as every story begins with exposition—a laying out of the ingredients that will make the main action possible—Book 13 is the exposition for the story of Odysseus's homecoming. It is also a figurative arming of the hero for his task—not arming with literal military equipment, but providing what Odysseus needs. What he needs most, we infer, is resourcefulness, hinted at when Athena calls him "a man never baffled" and refers to herself as having "a name among the gods for cleverness and intelligence" (Rouse translation). Part of the resourcefulness that Odysseus needs is the ability to maintain his disguise.

Athena is a somewhat enigmatic figure in *The Odyssey*. Although she is a goddess and sometimes exerts divine power, most of the time she seems more like a projection or personification of a mental quality, namely, Odysseus's cleverness or intelligence. Occasionally (including moments during her conversation with Odysseus in Book 13) she seems playful, whimsical, and teasing.

For Reflection or Discussion

As we experience the leave-taking from Phaiacia, we should ask how it provides a fitting conclusion to Odysseus's sojourn in this domestic utopia. Second, the relationship between "clever Odysseus" and Athena, goddess of wisdom and intelligence, is important to the story; what aspects of their relationship are reinforced in the conversation that takes place between them in Book 13? Finally, what things make up the game plan for Odysseus (aided by Athena) for the action that ensues?

BOOK 14

Odysseus and the Swineherd

Plot Summary

This is a low-voltage book with minimal action. As Odysseus approaches his house, the first person he encounters is his swineherd (one who looks after the hogs on the estate) named Eumaios ("u-MI-us"). The swineherd makes repeated displays of his loyalty to his absent master. He speaks well of Odysseus and laments the pillaging of his master's property. When the swineherd asks Odysseus who he is and where he has come from, Odysseus responds with a long, fabricated story having little relevance to the homecoming that is on our minds. After that, virtually everything that the swineherd does raises him in our estimation—and in Odysseus's estimation. He offers the first portions of meat to the gods. He is kind to the stranger before him. When Odysseus tests him by complaining that he is cold, the swineherd lends him his cloak.

Commentary

What's with the swineherd? we might be tempted to ask. There are good answers to that question. First, Eumaios will be a major player in the events that follow; Book 14 is our introduction to him. Additionally, it is part of Homer's design to display Odysseus's excellence as a ruler. The health of any society can be measured in part by how far down the social scale citizens "own" their country and display loyalty to it. The swineherd is at the bottom of his social scale and feels completely part of the enterprise.

Furthermore, ancient literature generally, and

The overall shape of the plot of *The Odyssey* is known as a comic plot—a U-shaped pattern in which events first descend into potential tragedy and then rise to a happy ending. As events move upward, obstacles to the happy ending are gradually removed. Further, in comic plots the hero is gradually integrated into society (whereas in tragedy the hero is progressively isolated from his society). Because *The Odyssey* is a return or homecoming story, the integration of the hero consists partly of his reunion with a series of people from whom he has been long separated. The swineherd is the first of these reunions.

Eumaios is one of Homer's most attractive minor characters. As is plainly evident in Book 14, a major ingredient in his positive characterization is his god-fearing piety. Numerous small details contribute to this religious note. A Christian reader can easily see the swineherd as a kindred spirit.

epic preeminently, show a class bias toward the aristocratic element in society. After all, epics were produced for the entertainment of the ruling warrior classes in their societies. But because *The Odyssey* is a domestic epic, it partly breaks the pattern in this regard. It portrays and celebrates the common as well as the aristocratic, and Book 14 is a prime example of the "simple people" principle.

Virtually every character in Ithaca (including the suitors) will have their loyalty tested by the disguised Odysseus. Most of the characters will fail the test. By passing his test with such distinction the swineherd will serve as a background foil to the other characters.

For Reflection or Discussion

First, what things make Eumaios the attractive character that literary critics have found him to be? Further, how does he indirectly contribute to the idealizing of Odysseus? Finally, what reminders does Book 14 provide of the chaos that has engulfed the kingdom of Odysseus in his absence?

BOOK 15

How Telemachos Sailed Back to Ithaca

The switch back to Telemachos in Sparta will be less of a jolt if we simply recall how familiar this technique is to storytelling. Here are the opening words of chapters 9–11 and 13 in C. S. Lewis's *The Lion, the Witch, and the Wardrobe*: "And now of course you want to know what had happened to Edmund"; "Now we must go back to Mr. and Mrs. Beaver and the three other children"; "Edmund meanwhile had been having a most disappointing time"; "Now we must get back to Edmund."

Plot Summary

Just when we thought we were headed for the climax of Odysseus's arrival home, Homer whisks us away to Sparta, where Athena finds Telemachos sound asleep in the palace of Menelaos. Suddenly we remember: the Telemachia had ended with the suitors plotting the death of Telemachos, but we had not actually seen Telemachos return to Ithaca. Athena instructs Telemachos to return to Ithaca at once, in a manner reminiscent of her visit early in the epic when she engineered the journey that Telemachos took to the mainland.

Telemachos obeys Athena's directives, and the next morning he leaves Sparta amid the usual round of hospitable giving and receiving of gifts. In an unexpected addition, just as the ship is ready to depart, a fugitive from justice named Theoclymenos asks to be taken onboard to Ithaca, and Telemachos gives his consent.

With Telemachos enroute to Ithaca, the second half of Book 15 shifts back to Odysseus and the swineherd. Odysseus tests the swineherd still further (we remember the incident of the cloak in the previous book) by offering to leave the swineherd's care and earn a living by working for the suitors. Eumaios passes the test by sternly warning against Odysseus's getting involved with the suitors. When Odysseus asks Eumaios to tell his life story, he obliges. It is a story of ill fortune until Eumaios was rescued and raised by Odysseus's father Laertes and his wife. The book ends with the arrival of Telemachos in Ithaca.

Commentary

The return to Telemachos in Sparta is actually a common storytelling strategy, though it has been so long since we have heard of Telemachos that we are momentarily mystified by the return to Sparta. When storytellers have two threads of action occurring simultaneously, they switch back and forth between them, in effect saying, "Now I need to bring you up to date about what is happening to character X."

Still, the introduction of such seemingly extraneous material as the background story of the fugitive Theoclymenos and the swineherd's autobiography can only be explained on the principle of epic embellishment. Epic storytellers love stories

The Odyssey is scattered with references to happenings in nature (usually involving birds) that are interpreted by characters in the story as omens or prophetic signs of what will happen soon. In Book 15, for example, an eagle carrying a goose stolen from a pen is interpreted by Helen as a sign that Odysseus is about to swoop down on the suitors and exact revenge. At such moments we need to operate in an awareness of what early in this guide ("The Author and His Faith") was called pagan analogues to the Christian faith. The omens are parallels to Christians' belief in divine providence and God's sometimes sending revelations to people.

and do not feel the novelist's impulse to keep the story they are telling sharply focused and unified.

Book 15 gives us yet more pictures of the hospitality code, all the way from leave-taking to welcoming of strangers to protecting vulnerable travelers. If one pieces together scattered pictures of hospitality from the Bible, the composite code of hospitality that emerges is close to what we see in *The Odyssey*; for details, see the article on hospitality in *Dictionary of Biblical Imagery* (InterVarsity, 1998).

Book 15 is built around the motifs of traveling and arriving home. Odysseus is a traveler who has finally arrived home. Telemachos travels by boat to his home. The story that Eumaios tells about his childhood life is a story of traveling until he reached Ithaca, where he found a home. A carefully contrived story like *The Odyssey* obeys an artistic principle known as "variations on a theme." Homer proved so good at the travel motif that he bequeathed our standard word *odyssey* to denote a journey.

For Reflection or Discussion

The overall direction in which the story is moving does not require the material that Homer put into Book 15; a good avenue toward analysis is to think of reasons why Homer included this book. Additionally, remembering that the ideal of worthy sons is important in *The Odyssey*, it is instructive to ponder parallels between Telemachos and Odysseus in Book 15. For example, both are recent arrivals in Ithaca; both participate in the code of hospitality, showing generosity as well as receiving it. How is Telemachos emerging as a son like his father?

BOOK 16

How Telemachos Met His Father

Plot Summary

The action in Book 16 occurs in three phases, each with its appropriate setting. The overall pattern is circular: from the swineherd's hut to the palace and back to the swineherd's hut.

The opening action is the reunion of Telemachos and the swineherd. It is a domestic scene, replete with hugging and crying. Of course there is irony in Telemachos's embracing a substitute father while his own father looks on. When Eumaios attempts to put the newly arrived stranger (Odysseus in disguise) under the care of Telemachos, Telemachos is suddenly overwhelmed by his sense of inadequacy to function as master in Ithaca. Odysseus enters the conversation, inquiring about family members and uttering sentiments designed to prompt Telemachos to take action against the suitors.

A third of the way through the book Athena appears, works a temporary transformation on Odysseus so that he appears in his true person and not as an old beggar, and directs Odysseus to reveal himself to his son. Father and son are duly reunited. Odysseus proceeds to outline a strategy for father and son to fight the suitors.

Without transition, halfway through the book the camera suddenly shifts to the suitors as they learn that Telemachos has returned safely to Ithaca. They propose a new plan to kill Telemachos, but one of their group (a nobleman who stands as a foil to the worst of the lot) proposes inquiring of the gods first. This proposal is accepted, and in a further resistance to the steamroller of evil, Penelope (having learned of the plot to kill her son) appears before the suitors and rebukes them. One of the suitors (Eurymachos) replies that Penelope has spoken wisely, but the narrator tells us that he said this only to quiet her while he was actually plotting murder.

At the end of the book one more important event remains. Odysseus needs to be disguised

Storytellers scarcely know how to tell a story without resorting to the technique of dramatic irony again and again. A good instance occupies us right here at the beginning of Book 16. The reunion between the swineherd and Telemachos is handled in terms of father-son reunion—while the real father looks on. To heighten the effect, Homer composes an epic simile in which he compares the reunion to a father son reunion: "As a father fondles the son whom he early loves . . . " Furthermore, Telemachos addresses the swineherd as his father.

The plans for future action that Odysseus doles out to Telemachos include ones that we might underestimate but that prove extremely important later. One is that Telemachos must restrain himself when he sees his father (disguised as an old beggar) mistreated by the suitors. A second is that Odysseus and Telemachos can have confidence that they, supported by the gods, can carry out their task against seemingly insurmountable odds. A third is that the weapons hanging on the walls of the great hall of the palace must be removed.

The justice motif will eventually come to dominate the action. It is important that we as readers are convinced that the suitors deserve the death that they receive from Odysseus and Telemachos. To that end, Homer includes many details, including speeches from the suitors themselves, to convict them in our eyes. An example is Penelope's rebuke to Antinoos, who turns out to be the ringleader of the evil suitors.

as a beggar during the conquest of the suitors. So Homer returns us to the swineherd's hut to witness Athena's transformation of Odysseus back into the guise of an old beggar.

Commentary

As readers we are eager to reach the climax of the story, but as noted previously, Homer is in no hurry to get there. His idea is to move us gradually toward the climax over the span of the second half of *The Odyssey*. So we need to settle down to relish the specific ways *by which* the story moves toward its climax and not be impatient to get only to *what happened* at the climax.

Storytellers absolutely love reunion scenes for the intensity of human emotion that they embody. The very nature of Homer's story will allow for a series of emotionally charged reunion scenes. The reunion between Odysseus and Telemachos is the first in the series.

Another of Homer's intentions with this book (and subsequent ones) is to keep the plot conflict between the villainous suitors and the family of Odysseus at a fever pitch right up to the slaughter of the suitors in the hall. This book keeps the conflict in our awareness.

Finally, Odysseus sets up some of the strategy that he and Telemachos will follow in the books that follow. Foremost among them are (a) the need to maintain the disguise of Odysseus and (b) trust in the sufficiency of divine help. On a more specific note, we learn along with Telemachos that when Odysseus gives him a nod in the hall he must remove the weapons from the walls and hide them in the upstairs storeroom.

For Reflection or Discussion

What localized features of the story told in Book 16 grab your attention? What elements of foreshadowing are important? What features keep the conflict between good and evil alive in our moral awareness?

BOOK 17

How Odysseus Returned to His Own Home

Plot Summary

The book opens with Telemachos instructing the swineherd to lead Odysseus, disguised as a beggar, to town. Telemachos himself goes home to be reunited with his mother after his secret journey. After this reunion, Telemachos goes to the marketplace to fetch a stranger named Theoclymenos, whom he had met on his journey to Pylos. When this pair arrives at Penelope's house, Penelope asks her son whether he has learned anything about his father. Telemachos replies that Menelaos had predicted that Odysseus would return and kill the suitors. The stranger, identified in the text as a prophet, confirms this prediction.

By now Odysseus has arrived in town, where the suitors appear at their absolute worst. In one vivid scene after another, the suitors abuse Odysseus in his disguise as a beggar. In a touching detail, Odysseus's dog recognizes his returned master but dies before he can give Odysseus's identity away. The scene shifts to the great hall (the dining hall of the palace), where mealtime provides an occasion

Because of the disguise of Odysseus, the discrepancy between appearance and reality will be a main technique employed by Homer in this phase of the story. The literary term for this is of course *dramatic irony*. In addition to the obvious examples of such ironic discrepancy, there are subtle ones, and in keeping with epic technique, the narrator tells us what we need to know in these instances. For example, early in Book 17 the narrator tells us that Penelope did not know what Telemachos meant when he spoke of a day of reckoning in regard to the arrival of the stranger (Odysseus in disguise), and just a few lines later the narrator tells us that the suitors crowded around Telemachos with pleasant words but with hatred in their hearts. This clarifying role of the narrator will become important in the interpretation of later books, especially in regard to the question of when Penelope comes to recognize the beggar as Odysseus.

It is important that we duly register the repeated small moments of foreshadowing that Homer put into this part of the story. A prophet's prediction that Odysseus is at hand, the report of omens by the same prophet, a sneeze interpreted as evidence that Odysseus will return—small details like these add up to a total picture. The question of exactly when Penelope realizes that the beggar is her husband will become an important interpretive question in Book 22; by the time we reach that point, there have been enough hints that something is afoot in Ithaca for us to conclude that Penelope does not totally rule out the possibility of her husband's return.

Epic is known for its formality and its high style, consisting of such things as stately epithets and rhetorically embellished speeches. Homer does not disappoint us in this regard. But Homer's realism and love of the sharply delineated detail from real life are also legendary. In Book 17 Homer gives us abundant examples of such

for further mistreatment of the beggar. Penelope expresses a wish to converse with the stranger, but Homer removes her from the scene so as to delay the climactic reunion between Odysseus and Penelope.

Commentary

We are in a section of the epic where everything is moving slowly—slowly—toward the final showdown. The elements of foreshadowing are numerous. An example is an early comment that the mind of Telemachos was full of the coming fight. Or a passing wish by Penelope that the prophet's prediction that Odysseus is home might be fulfilled. Again, late in the book when Telemachos sneezes, Penelope interprets it (laughingly, to be sure) as evidence that death will come on the intruders. The cumulative weight of these statements is to intensify our awareness that events are moving toward their climax.

Dramatic irony complements foreshadowing as the mainspring of action in Book 17. The insolent intruders who appear at their very worst are in effect signing their own death warrant, but only we know that. The suitors themselves have no inkling that the beggar is Odysseus. The audience is intended to relish this ironic discrepancy between their superior knowledge and the suitor's ignorance of the true situation.

Third, the justice motif continues to be important. Homer wants us to see and hear and feel the evil represented by the suitors. If we do not experience the images of evil at their full force, our moral sense will not be satisfied when the slaughter occurs.

For Reflection or Discussion

An appropriate subtitle for Book 17 would be "images of evil and barbarity." A good way to progress through the book is to make a mental note of the examples of this evil and barbarity. For you personally, what is the most vivid moment in Book 17? Additionally, what are the most important moments of foreshadowing and of dramatic irony?

realism—a kick on the hip, a vermin-covered dog lying on a heap of cow dung, a footstool hurled at Odysseus and landing on the back under his right shoulder, and more.

How Odysseus Fought the Sturdy Beggar

Plot Summary

"Are we there yet?" small children ask incessantly on car trips. "Are we there yet?" we ask Homer. His reply is that he is in no hurry to get to the climax of the story. Book 18 narrates events that are hardly required for the main plotline. Our task is to figure out what Homer's strategy is.

The opening scenario is a fight between the established town beggar and Odysseus in the guise of a beggar. At stake is who will be allowed the right to beg on the property of Odysseus. Odysseus mangles his challenger in an action that should have warned the onlooking suitors, but they remain oblivious to the meaning of the event. When Odysseus discourses on human vulnerability to one of the suitors, the suitor is troubled by what he experiences as foreboding.

The second main event is Penelope's appearance in the hall. All eyes are on her as she chastises Telemachos for not establishing order in the house.

The behavior of the veteran beggar on the premises is one of the most vivid instances of disorder that we have seen. The function of the beggar is partly to evoke our revulsion toward what is happening in Odysseus's house. Additionally, if the suitors represent chaos from without, the behavior of the beggar and the maid represent domestic chaos from within the familiar household. So does the spectacle of the suitors thinking that watching a brawl is great entertainment.

Telemachos manages to placate her, and she turns to conversation with a suitor named Eurymachos. She hints that the time is approaching where she will need to marry one of the suitors, who for once behave like suitors and give Penelope gifts.

In the last third of the book, Odysseus interacts with servants and selected suitors, who implicitly determine their eventual fate at the hands of Odysseus. A maid named Melantho insults Odysseus. Athena prompts Eurymachos to rudeness as well. In fact, he matches an earlier event in the hall by hurling a footstool at Odysseus. In a note of foreshadowing, Telemachos calls the room to order with dignity, leading the suitors to bite their lips when they observe his confidence.

Homer's skill with realistic description is never far from the surface. The vividness with which the damage that Odysseus inflicts on the body of the beggar who challenges him is a small classic in this vein. So is the prize for winning the fight: a lot of black puddings stuffed with blood and fat.

Commentary

A continuing piece of "narrative business" is to continue to fill out the picture of social disorder at the palace of Odysseus. What has engulfed the palace of Odysseus is not simply a bit of social impropriety; it is a blow at civilization itself as barbarism descends like the night. Fighting between two beggars is the first example. Insurrection in the form of Melantho's sassiness to her master is a second example. The flying footstool is a third. We are led to understand that every corner of household life has been infiltrated by disorder.

Foreshadowing also continues apace. The thoroughness of Odysseus's defeat of the rival beggar is an example of his tremendous strength in combat. Another example occurs when Odysseus "talks out of the side of his mouth" to Amphinomos about how people who disregard justice are asking for trouble. A similar moment occurs late in the book when Odysseus makes a prediction of what will happen "if Odysseus should come back to his native land."

A third motif emerges if we pay attention to the details. The overall story of Telemachos in *The Odyssey* is an initiation or coming-of-age story. There are hints of Telemachos's growing maturity in Book 18. Penelope's criticism of Telemachos for not protecting the stranger is a test of Telemachos's ability not to interfere with Odysseus's disguise. Telemachos responds by answering "with his usual good sense" (Rouse translation). At the end, when Telemachos brings order to the chaotic situation, the suitors are surprised by his confidence.

For Reflection or Discussion

The foregoing commentary lays down the right lines of inquiry. What telling details add to the indictment of the suitors? What details foreshadow the coming showdown between Odysseus and the suitors? How can we chart Telemachos's growth in maturity?

Although critics are divided on the question of when Penelope determines that the beggar is her husband, the cumulative evidence that collects over a span of several books is that she is divided in her opinion regarding whether Odysseus is dead or whether she should continue to hold out hope. In Book 18 she expresses the sentiment that she is ready to marry one of the suitors.

BOOK 19

How the Old Nurse Knew Her Master

Plot Summary

Are we there yet? Not in the least. Homer wants us to meander toward the climax, not gallop toward it. In an important piece of foreshadowing, the nurse is told to shut the female servants in their rooms while Odysseus and Telemachos remove the armor from the great hall. When Penelope

The invocation at the very beginning of *The Odyssey* called Odysseus a man never at a loss (or an equivalent, depending on the translation). The narrator loves the epithet "clever Odysseus." Book 19 contains numerous evidences of Odysseus's cleverness. This is how we should interpret the opening event of removing the armor from the hall, whereas otherwise the suitors could grab it when Odysseus and Telemachos attack them.

We can also relish Odysseus's quickness of mind in the conversations with Penelope. At one point the epic narrator makes Odysseus's mental adroitness explicit when he says that Odysseus must have all his wits about him as he interacts with Penelope. Odysseus does a masterful job of keeping Penelope's hopes alive, without, however, giving her reason to believe just yet that her husband has returned or that he will defeat the suitors.

arrives on the scene, she observes Melantho treating Odysseus rudely yet again.

There follows a leisurely exchange between Penelope and Odysseus—not the *ultimate* conversation between them, but a preliminary one. With the disguised Odysseus situated in a domestic scene (replete with rug and chair), Penelope asks him to tell the story of who he is. Odysseus evades her question, so she confides in the stranger about her situation. It is, as we know, a story of distress. Odysseus-as-beggar then claims to have seen Odysseus on his travels, and when he describes the very clothes that he himself wore, Penelope weeps. Odysseus claims further that he has heard a rumor that Penelope's husband is near home.

The second half of Book 19 is devoted to one of the really famous scenes in *The Odyssey*. The action consists of an old family nurse named Eurycleia bathing Odysseus in his disguise as a beggar. As a child, Odysseus had received a scar from an attack by a wild boar, and as a longstanding family servant Eurycleia recognizes Odysseus when she touches the scar while bathing his feet. As Eurycleia turns to share the news with her mistress, Odysseus grabs her by the throat and tells her not to inform Penelope. Did Penelope see what happened? No: the narrator tells us plainly that she noticed nothing.

Following the bath, Penelope again confides in the beggar. Although there are omens and signs that something is moving toward a culmination in regard to her husband, Penelope is unable to believe with certainty that Odysseus will return. Nonetheless, Odysseus-as-beggar encourages Penelope to follow through with her proposal to set up a shooting contest for the suitors.

Commentary

Book 19 springs a wealth of complexity on us, after several books in which the narrative business was simple and straightforward. Early and late in the book, Penelope is surprisingly open with the stranger (Odysseus in disguise) about her situation. If we put all of Penelope's statements together into a composite picture, it is evident that she is ambivalent about whether Odysseus will return. Some of the things that she says—and some of the data that she adduces—add up to a picture of openness at least to believe that her husband might return. Other statements paint a picture of despair about the possibility of such a return. Overall, Penelope is indecisive and of two minds.

Meanwhile, what is the game plan of Odysseus? He does not want his wife to give up hope before he has made an end of the suitors, but it is also his intention to delay his revelation of himself until after he has defeated the suitors. That is the best interpretation of the data that Homer puts before us in Book 19.

In the middle of the book, we are asked to relish the story of how the nurse recognized her master of long ago. The human intensity of the scene is hard to beat, especially the nurse's response in her moment of discovery.

What are we to make of the shooting contest that Penelope has considered staging? In the background lies a practice of using a shooting contest as a prenuptial ritual to decide who gets to marry the eligible woman. In the version that we encounter in *The Odyssey,* whoever can string the bow and shoot an arrow through the openings of twelve axes will get to marry Penelope. Why does Odysseus encourage Penelope to stage the contest? We need to read

There have been some super-subtle interpretations of Book 19 that assert that Penelope comes to recognize that the beggar is her husband. On this reading, Penelope and Odysseus speak a kind of code language in which they signal to each other that they know that Penelope has recognized Odysseus, and in which they set up the ground rules for the slaughter of the suitors in the hall. It is much more plausible to conclude that Penelope does, indeed, come to put a degree of trust in the beggar as a source of information about her husband but that she never entertains the possibility that the beggar actually *is* her husband.

between the lines: only Odysseus is strong enough to string the bow, so the contest is in effect a delaying strategy, allowing Odysseus to kill the suitors before Penelope needs to marry one of them.

For Reflection or Discussion

What details paint a picture of Penelope's having given up on the possibility of her husband's return? What details paint a contradictory picture that Penelope hopes that Odysseus will return?

BOOK 20

How God Sent Omens of the Wrath to Come

Plot Summary

"Are we there yet?" we ask Homer. His reply: "Oh, no, I have a lot of good story material that I can't bear to omit, and besides, I want to delay the climax." Book 20 is a book of foreshadowing in which the chief narrative business is to add still more to the case against the suitors. The book is a kaleidoscope of details unified by a crescendo of buildup to the climactic battle.

We begin with a nighttime scene in which Odysseus hears his female servants going off to their customary sexual activities and then lies awake. Athena comes to him in a vision, and he asks how he can manage the battle against the suitors against such impossible odds. Penelope also has dreams in her troubled sleep. An omen in the form of a thunderclap gives Odysseus hope for the day's ordeal.

Part of Homer's genius in *The Odyssey* is that he keeps revealing more and more levels of disorder brought into the palace of Odysseus by the suitors. An example is the opening picture in Book 20 of the female servants giggling and joking as they make their nightly visit to their lovers. Homer's strategy is to build up such a strong sense of revulsion against the villains of the story that no possibility of sympathy for them should arise when they are executed.

If we read with an awareness that this is the big day, we experience the details as we experience the momentous days in our own lives. On such days, everything is laden with significance. Thus we have snapshots of animals being herded for slaughter to feed the suitors; Telemachos choosing a place for Odysseus-as-beggar in the hall and telling the suitors to behave themselves; Athena provoking the suitors to mistreat Odysseus. When a cow's foot is flung at Odysseus, Telemachos stands up to the suitors, declaring that he is "no longer a child" but sees what is going on. The suitors belittle Telemachos, but Athena sends an omen in the form of their plates being messed with blood and tears streaming from their eyes. The final snapshot is memorable: Telemachos looking toward his father, and Penelope seated outside the door of the hall and overhearing everything.

Commentary

The key to relishing this book is to regard it as the first of a block of three books designed to move us with an ever-increasing sense of anticipation to the climax of the battle in the hall. With that as a framework, we can notice how Homer's imagination worked in choosing the details that he thought would evoke the greatest anticipation. To fill out the picture of moral disorder, Homer gives us snapshots of promiscuous women of Odysseus's court, the faithful goatherd's comment that God's wrath doesn't make the suitors tremble, a flying cow's foot intended to hit Odysseus (disguised as a beggar), and a key speech by Telemachos in which he speaks of violence at the palace, strangers knocked about, and women dragged all over the place in an indecent way.

Another thing that Homer does well in Book 20 is to keep us updated on how the members of Odysseus's family are behaving under the pressure of what we know is about to happen. Thus we have Odysseus's anxiety dream about how he can be successful in fighting so many opponents, Penelope's anxiety dream about needing to declare her husband dead and marry one of the suitors, and at the end Telemachos looking at his father in silence, biding his time. It is as though Homer is telling us a story of public events and a private family history at the same time.

One of Homer's ways of belittling the suitors in our estimate is to make them obtuse or slow on the draw when confronted with data that should have been interpreted as a warning to them. When Odysseus easily mangles the beggar who has challenged him to a fight (Book 18), the suitors laugh uproariously. Here in Book 20, when the prophet Theoclymenos utters oracles of warning to the suitors, they laugh and tease Telemachos about his guests. The effect is that the suitors emerge in our estimate as being stupid as well as evil.

An additional motif is the omens that Homer inserts into the flow. Examples include the thunderclap that a woman grinding at the mill hears, an eagle flying with a trembling dove in his claws, the appearance of blood on the plates of the suitors, and others.

For Reflection or Discussion

The lens through which we should read Book 20 is the lens of premonition or foreshadowing. The items mentioned in the commentary section above are only a beginning. Many more deserved to be tabulated in our minds and imaginations.

BOOK 21

The Contest with the Great Bow

Plot Summary

The contest with the bow is obviously an important part of Homer's design. Among other things, the bow will be what Odysseus uses to start the battle against the suitors. We are intended to relish the leisurely dispensing of information in the opening moments of Book 21.

The tension continues to build, and Homer gets as much mileage as possible out of the technique of gradual approach to the climax. The chief vehicle by which he pursues that game plan in Book 21 is the shooting contest. Right at the outset Homer tells us that the contest was Penelope's way of getting her husband's great bow into the hall. The ground rules for the contest are two: a contestant must first string the bow and then shoot an arrow through twelve axes. The axes probably were in the shape of the English letter P, and the round space in the top was the part through which the arrow needed to pass. Penelope says that whoever can meet the two prerequisites will marry her.

There is an element of comedy in the futile attempts of the suitors to string the bow. Readers familiar with the Bible might well recall the parallel situation of the prophets of Baal on Mount Carmel, making fools of themselves as they tried to call down fire from heaven. In the middle of the story of the suitors' frustration, Homer inserts the incident of Odysseus's revelation of his identity to the swineherd and the drover (one who drives sheep and cattle from one place to another) so that they can help in the battle against the suitors.

The final key event in the movement toward the battle in the hall comes when Odysseus, disguised as an old beggar, asks to try his hand with the bow. The suitors object, but Penelope speaks on behalf of the beggar. Telemachos then intervenes and claims the right to give the bow to the beggar, directing his mother to go to her room. She does so, and the book ends with Odysseus's easily stringing the bow, twanging the string, and shooting the arrow through the tops of the axes.

Commentary

The chief things that require interpretation are the nature of the shooting contest and more specifically the stringing of the bow. The following is a consensus of scholarly opinion. The contest is a prenuptial competition, a motif with roots in folklore. In the folktale versions of the story, the understood premise is that only the hero of the story is strong enough to string the bow. If this is the premise in *The Odyssey*, Penelope knows that none of the suitors can string the bow, so she is actually deceiving them and carrying out a clever delaying strategy. Confirmation of this interpretation comes at the end of the book when Odysseus easily strings the bow, leaving the suitors dumbfounded.

Telemachos twice comes close to stringing the

Another motif that is nearing completion in *The Odyssey* is the growing maturity of Telemachos. Book 21 is filled with hints of this. For example, when Telemachos sets up the twelve axes in a row, we read that all of the suitors were surprised to see how expertly he did it, even though he had never seen the axes before. Many similar moments occur in Book 21 as Telemachos grows in stature with nearly every move.

Another thing that contributes to the mounting sense of anticipation is various strategy moves that Odysseus makes. For example, he not only informs the herd driver and swineherd of his identity but also sets up a signal for the swineherd to put the bow in Odysseus's hands and bolt the doors to the women's rooms. Many such details make Book 21 a grand planning session for a military operation.

When the suitors object to Penelope's instruction to let the visiting beggar try to string the bow, she proposes an alternate prize to marrying her if the beggar strings the bow. This should be taken at face value: a beggar was not in the running to marry an aristocratic lady.

Book 21 ends with some of the most memorable pictures in the entire *Odyssey*. Examples include Odysseus's making the string of the bow twang and sing like a swallow; a confirming omen from Zeus in the form of a thunderclap; the arrow flying straight through the tops of the axes; the understatement from Odysseus to Telemachos that his guest is no discredit to him; the grim irony of Odysseus's saying that it is time to prepare supper and entertainment for the company of suitors; Telemachos standing armed by his father's side. In the annals of storytelling, it is hard to beat this.

bow and is certain that he can do it on the third try, but Odysseus gives him a sign not to try. In this we are to see that the initiation of Telemachos and his maturation into a worthy son are almost complete.

If we accept what is stated above, the suitors' foolish attempts to string the bow are another example of dramatic irony. Book 21 unfolds as a comic put-down of the suitors, who emerge in our imaginations as a bunch of weaklings despite their assertive behavior in taking over Odysseus's palace.

Another interpretive crux in *The Odyssey* is the question of when Penelope becomes aware that the beggar is actually her husband. The approach taken in this guide is that Homer artfully delays the reunion between Odysseus and Penelope until Book 23. If we look carefully at the relevant passages in Book 21, it is evident that Homer manages the action so as to maintain the continuing ignorance of Penelope regarding the identity of Odysseus. One example among many occurs when Telemachos tells his mother to retire to her room, thereby removing Penelope from the battle in the hall; we read that "by grace of Athena she fell into a sound sleep" (Rouse translation).

For Reflection or Discussion

The main narrative business of Book 21 is to intensify our sense of anticipation regarding the coming climax (the battle in the hall). What notes of foreshadowing and growing anticipation press themselves into our awareness as we read? What details show how Homer orchestrates the continuing unawareness of Penelope in regard to the identity of the beggar? How does Book 21 emerge as another triumph of ironic technique in the late stages of the story?

BOOK 22

The Battle in the Hall

Plot Summary

Are we there yet? Yes, we have finally arrived. This should not subvert the importance of what happens in the last two books of *The Odyssey*, but the plotline has been moving inexorably toward retribution against the suitors for their unspeakable evil. The stage for the suitors' defeat was set at the end of Book 21 when Odysseus easily strung the bow and shot the arrow through the axe heads and when he nodded to Telemachos to get ready. In Book 22 the battle begins with Odysseus's sending an arrow into the throat of Antinoos (worst of the worst) as he was caught in a symbolic moment of holding a goblet in his hands. Although the suitors initially think this is a bit of misconduct from the beggar, Odysseus announces his identity and makes a formal statement of charges.

After that we get a blow-by-blow account of the battle and its fluctuations (all good battle stories have back-and-forth changes of fortune). The almost-mature Telemachos makes a costly mistake by not locking the door to the store room, thereby allowing the suitors to fetch the previously stowed weapons. But the army of four (father and son plus the two farm hands) gradually gains the ascendency. Although the dominant force of Book 22 is justice, Odysseus honors his son's plea to show mercy toward the court poet (whose innocence is asserted). The female servants who had participated in the moral chaos at the palace are executed after being forced to clean up the mess in the hall.

For the cultures that produced ancient epics, warfare was a common feature of life. All audiences expect at least some of the literature that they assimilate to portray the details of their own experiences. Homer honors that expectation in abundance in Book 22. The battle emerges in full detail in our imaginations.

Epic is a bigger-than-life genre. The genres of myth and fantasy dominate epics. But paradoxically Homer is also famous for the minute realism of his stories. Passage after passage in Book 22 adheres to the conventions of literary realism—the impulse to portray life (especially the physical details of life) in photographic realism. In Book 22, that realism consists especially of the bodily sensations of injury and death in battle.

Many aspects of the initiation of Telemachos into mature adulthood draw upon familiar rituals found in both literature and life. Homer's original audience was probably just waiting for the almost-mature young hero to make a notable mistake on the verge of his full maturity. The failure of Telemachos to lock the storeroom door gave the audience what it was expecting.

In keeping with the religious orientation of Homer's worldview, the goddess Athena plays an important role in the battle in the hall. She prods Odysseus to military feats. She controls the progress of the battle in such a way as to allow Telemachos to demonstrate his prowess. She makes the arrows of the suitors miss their mark. All of this has a familiar feel to anyone who knows the Old Testament stories of the interaction between divine providence and human effort in the Old Testament historical chronicles.

A series of three epic similes highlights the progress of the battle. The suitors are progressively compared to (a) a herd of cows scampering to get away from flies, (b) a flock of birds attacked by vultures, and (c) a haul of fishes drawn in by a fisherman's net. The stature and fortunes of the suitors shrink before us as Homer assembles these epic similes.

Commentary

The most important thing to acknowledge as we read Book 22 is that the theme of *The Odyssey* is not mercy but justice. Justice is a moral ideal and an attribute that the Bible ascribes to God. This is a way of saying that we should not feel apologetic about justice when it is administered, nor should any sympathy flow toward the suitors, who have been given numerous opportunities and appeals to reform their behavior as the story unfolded. Additionally, we must understand that in ancient times the exacting of justice was administered privately by the person who had been aggrieved. There was no court of justice or trial by jury. So what looks like personal revenge should be understood as the serving of justice on the guilty.

For readers of refined sensibilities, the emphasis on the physical sensations of combat and killing will doubtless be a deterrent to relishing the account of the slaughter in the hall. We can exercise our historical imaginations in the matter and understand that warfare was a way of life for Homer's culture and in ancient times generally. *The Odyssey* devotes just one book to the type of military action that was the chief story material of most epics.

Book 22 will also seem more familiar if we realize that similar action is narrated in Old Testament historical chronicles. Old Testament stories of warfare conducted to execute justice and vengeance for the stealing of property and damage done to one's family include Abraham's pursuit of the kings who had pillaged and kidnapped his nephew Lot and others (Genesis 14, an epic episode) and David's exacting of revenge when his possessions and wives were carried off by the Amalekites (1 Samuel 30).

For Reflection or Discussion

The impressionistic question of what stands out most as we assimilate Book 22 is a good starting point for reflection or discussion. Second, it is important to cast a retrospective look at the entire epic up to this point and recollect the cumulative weight of the case against the suitors and the extent of their monstrosity. Finally, beyond the simple fact that without justice, civilization in a fallen world destroys itself, we can reflect on justice as an attribute and activity of the God of the Bible; relevant parallel passages from the Psalms include the following: 7:9–17; 37:27–29; 72:1–4; 82; 96:10–13.

Penelope is carefully excluded from the action. When the nurse Eurycleia wishes to summon her mistress, Odysseus tells her not to wake Penelope yet. Then the hall is purged and disinfected. Only then is Eurycleia allowed to request Penelope to come to the hall.

BOOK 23

How Odysseus Found His Wife Again

Plot Summary

The focus of this book is the reunion of Penelope and her husband. As earlier parts of this guide have noted, Homer has kept the question of when Penelope knows that the beggar is her husband on the radar screen throughout the second half of the epic. Although scholarly opinion is not unanimous in accepting this view, it is the majority viewpoint. Homer signals that this is his intention right at the beginning of Book 23: Eurycleia announces that Odysseus is in the house, but we read that Penelope was too cautious to believe this.

The rest of Book 23 is an exercise in persuasion. First the nurse assembles data that would allow Penelope to conclude that Odysseus is home.

As we witness Penelope's ongoing skepticism about the claims that the beggar is Odysseus, we need to keep in our minds that Penelope was not a witness to the battle in the hall. Earlier sections of this guide drew attention to places in the preceding books of the epic where the epic narrator made explicit statements to show that Penelope was deprived of information that might have led her to recognize the beggar. In Book 23, too, the epic narrator is a helpful travel guide, telling us that "Penelope was too cautious to believe this," or that "Penelope still doubtful replied."

The marriage bed that Odysseus built symbolizes much about his marriage. Odysseus built the bed by himself; it is his and Penelope's secret. The fact that the bedpost is a tree symbolizes the fixedness and stability of the marriage and also signals Odysseus's emancipation from his wanderings.

The marriage bed has been a unifying image in *The Odyssey.* Brief pictures of couples lying down in bed at night have punctuated the action. The final appearance of this motif comes when Odysseus says, "But come to your bed, my wife, that we may have the delight of sleeping side by side."

Odysseus's story of his wanderings as told to Penelope serves the function of reminding us of the price that Odysseus paid to reach the reunion that we have just witnessed. Additionally, we can scrutinize Odysseus's account for interpretive clues that shed light on the twelve adventures. An example is when he says that Calypso promised to make him immortal.

Then Odysseus makes an appearance and scolds Penelope for not accepting him as her husband. Penelope herself arranges the climactic proof when she asks Eurycleia to make her bed outside the bedroom. Odysseus erupts at this because he himself had made the bed with a tree as one of the bedposts. Husband and wife are thereupon reunited. The second half of the book is devoted to a summary of Odysseus's recounting the events in his journey home. At the very end of the book, Odysseus suddenly announces that he must visit his father (who, as we learned earlier in the epic, lives in forlorn solitude), and he puts on his armor in preparation, taking Telemachos with him.

Commentary

Although the battle in the hall is the climax of the plot of *The Odyssey*, it is important not to over-emphasize this facet of the story. Books 23 and 24 transact important narrative and (even more) thematic business. Both books deal with the reuniting of long-separated family members. Book 23 is rightly regarded as the climax of the marital motif in *The Odyssey.* Viewed from this domestic angle, the slaughter in the hall was the enabling action for the completion of the family concerns that motivated the homeward journey of Odysseus.

The key to following the action as it unfolds in Book 23 is to operate on the premise that first, Penelope needs to be persuaded that the beggar is her husband. Only after her resistance is conquered is the reconciliation possible. Further, Penelope is of two minds in the first half of the book. She never totally rejects the possibility that the beggar is Odysseus; she simply remains unconvinced. So we can trace the back-and-forth vacillation going on in Penelope's mind as Eurycleia and Odysseus present data to her.

Storytellers absolutely love reunion scenes because of the emotional potential that they contain. Once Penelope's doubt is conquered, Book 23 becomes a grand reunion story. Parallel stories from Genesis include the reunion of Jacob and Esau (Gen. 33:1–14) and the reunion of Joseph and his brothers (Genesis 45).

For Reflection or Discussion

What passages create an overall picture of Penelope as a case study in doubt or skepticism in the first half of the book? Throughout the epic, Odysseus is touted as "clever Odysseus," the man never at a loss; how does Penelope emerge in Book 23 as a worthy wife to clever Odysseus? How does the reunion of Odysseus and Penelope serve as an emotional resting place for the entire story that has preceded?

Some readers wonder why at the end of Book 23 Homer suddenly interrupts the reunion scene and propels Odysseus and Telemachos into further military action. It is true that Odysseus has reclaimed his wife and home, but (a) Odysseus has a public role as well as a private one, and (b) home in *The Odyssey* means kingdom as well as family. Additionally, family implies parent as well as wife and son, hence the reunion of Odysseus with his father Laertes.

BOOK 24

How Odysseus Found His Old Father and How the Story Ended

Plot Summary

Book 24 falls into three sections and is filled with surprises. The first surprise occurs right at the outset, as we are whisked away (and without explanation) to the abode of the dead. Our visit there begins with an exchange between Achilles and Agamemnon. Agamemnon tells Achilles about

Although Book 22 (the slaughter in the hall) is the only extended bow that Homer makes to the martial theme of classical epic, we are given glimpses of the heroic code and military ethos throughout *The Odyssey.* The dialogue between Achilles and Agamemnon is one of the most memorable pictures of the heroic code that we get in this epic. Additionally, the story of Agamemnon's death at the hand of a treacherous wife has served as background chorus to the main melodic line of Odysseus's return to his faithful wife.

Following the account from one of the suitors about how Odysseus returned home, Agamemnon responds with an emotional exclamation that encapsulates much of the story of Odysseus. He calls Odysseus someone who is ready for every danger (a variation on the theme of the clever hero). But Agamemnon lavishes most of his attention on Penelope. Agamemnon is right: ultimately Odysseus owes the happiness of his return to the faithfulness of his wife.

how famous he is in the land of the living, and about how impressive his funeral was. This bit of dialogue is followed by the arrival of the souls of the suitors slain by Odysseus. One of them dispassionately tells the complete story of their defeat by Odysseus. Agamemnon responds by paying tribute to Penelope as the supreme blessing in Odysseus's life.

With that preliminary action complete, Homer turns to the action that was foreshadowed at the end of Book 23—Odysseus's visit to his father Laertes. We had already been given a picture of a forlorn Laertes living a life of seclusion on a farm. Instead of immediately revealing who he is, Odysseus spins a fabricated story about who he is and how he has arrived in Ithaca. But eventually Odysseus relents, and another emotional family reunion occurs.

Then in a completely different vein, and again without transition, we read about how the friends and relatives of the slain suitors held a meeting in the wake of the defeat of the suitors. Part of the assembly decides to form an army and attack Odysseus. This, in turn, allows for a memorable picture of Odysseus and Telemachos—father and worthy son—to stand beside each other in armor, poised for battle. But Athena, voice of wisdom, intervenes, and the story quickly ends with a declaration of peace.

Commentary

Several things are at work in the opening scene set in the underworld. To begin, Achilles and Agamemnon represent a picture of heroism as the epic tradition understands it—warriors who have become famous through their military exploits.

Within that commonality, these two heroes are foils to each other. They both died, but Achilles died a heroic death on the battlefield, while Agamemnon died an inglorious death at the hand of a faithless wife and her lover. Into the world of true heroism comes the procession of ignominious suitors, who died an ignoble death of deserved retribution.

The middle scenario in Book 24 is much more plausible as an element in the story. The Odyssey is a homecoming story. We expect to see Odysseus reunited with his father as well as his wife and son. The forlorn state in which Laertes has lived for years is a foil to his joy at learning that his son is alive and home.

But what are we to make of the unexpected addition of the final skirmish between the survivors of the dead suitors and Odysseus? It is partly a picture of the sheer persistence of evil—the refusal of biased people to acknowledge the deserved deaths of their loved ones. But probably the main purpose of the episode is to bring the initiation of Telemachos to its climax, as Telemachos proves himself a worthy son—a rival in courage to his father, as Laertes exclaims.

For Reflection or Discussion

A profitable initial exercise is simply to note what surprises us in Book 24. Then we should come up with plausible explanations of why Homer sprung those surprises on his audience. Another avenue toward analysis is to ponder how Book 24 reminds us of big effects in The Odyssey as a whole, allowing us to put it all together here at the end. Finally, Odysseus is one of the most famous literary heroes of Western literature; how does Book 24 serve as a summary of his character and roles?

Odysseus's stringing his father along with a fabricated story instead of immediately being reunited with him aligns Odysseus with an archetype known as the wily lad. That side of Odysseus's personality has been evident throughout the story and is hinted at in the epithet "clever Odysseus." The wily lad has a knack for getting himself into difficulty. He is overly curious (the "Curious George" type). In fact, he has a mischievous side and seems to delight in carrying out deceit. There were moments on the homeward voyage when Odysseus was his own worst enemy.

The Odyssey in Biblical Perspective

Almost every major genre and archetype found in *The Odyssey* finds parallels in the Bible, and Homer's story can profitably be set alongside its biblical counterparts. Archetypes such as the hero, the quest, homecoming, the worthy son, the ideal wife, testing, temptation, and the sea are examples of shared archetypes between *The Odyssey* and the Bible. Genres are also shared: travel story, battle story, story of hospitality, initiation story, return story, recognition story, etc. The definitive reference book on these archetypes and genres is *Dictionary of Biblical Imagery*, edited by Leland Ryken and others (Downers Grove, IL: InterVarsity, 1998). For anyone wishing to place Homer's story into a context of biblical parallels, this is the essential source.

The Odyssey is a domestic epic. The most obvious biblical parallels are the domestic stories of Abraham (Genesis 12–25) and Ruth. These two epic-like stories make excellent collaborative reading for *The Odyssey*.

At a thematic level too, *The Odyssey* shares many preoccupations with the writers of the Bible. Examples include the ideal of faithful and permanent married love, the importance of home and family, life as a test that requires choice of good over evil, the nature of people (capable of both good and evil), the certainty of justice, and the importance of hospitality. *The Odyssey* gives us many pictures of the good life; so does the Bible (see the article on "good life" in *Dictionary of Biblical Imagery*). Of course Homer did not know about the God of the Bible or the Christian religion, so there are differences as well as similarities to be noted.

Whereas the worldview of Homer falls notably short of the Christian worldview (especially in the areas of the nature of God and the centrality of the forgiveness of sins through the atonement of Christ), the *morality* of *The Odyssey*—the scheme of virtues and vices—is largely consonant with Christian morality. By God's common grace, Homer got it right in regard to the ideal of faithful and permanent wedded love, the importance of a harmonious and well-ordered family, the need for self-control in the face of temptations, and reverence toward the divine.

The Bible itself provides a model for being positive about the partial truthfulness of Greek literature. In the New Testament, Paul several times quotes with approval from Greek authors (Acts 17:28; 1 Cor. 15:23; Titus 1:12, where Paul follows the quotation with the comment, "This statement is true"). The Titus passage led John Calvin to articulate the doctrine of common grace thus: "All truth is from God; and consequently, if wicked men have said anything that is true and just, we ought not to reject it; for it has come from God."

Tie-Ins with the Book of Proverbs

There are several things that make the Old Testament book of Proverbs good collaborative reading for *The Odyssey*. The first is that these two books share many of the same preoccupations. The attitude that the respective authors take toward these shared interests is also often identical. An inquiry into the social context will help to explain why the agreement exists. C. S. Lewis described ancient epic as "poetry *about* nobles [aristocrats], made *for* nobles." Old Testament Wisdom Literature (which was actually an international phenomenon in its day) was also a courtly genre—a form of court instruction for future rulers. Below is a partial tabulation of passages from the book of Proverbs (arranged topically) that codify leading aspects of *The Odyssey*.

- The value and attributes of a worthy wife: 12:4; 18:22; 19:14; 31:10–31.
- The value of having or being a worthy son: 10:1; 15:20; 23:15, 24; 27:11.
- The dangers of forbidden sex and the ideal of faithful wedded love: 2:16–19; 5:1–6, 15–20; 6:23–29, 32; chapter 7.
- The importance and exalted status of wisdom (in *The Odyssey* Athena is the goddess of wisdom): 1:20–33; chapter 2; 4:1–13.
- The self-destructiveness of living by violence, and the need to avoid casting one's lot with the violent wicked: 1:8–19; 3:31–32; 21:7; 24:1–2, 15–16.
- The certainty of judgment against the wicked: 2:21–22; 11:21, 23; 12:7; 13:21; 21:6–8; 22:8.
- The joy that comes when the wicked fall: 11:10; 21:15; 28:5.
- Reward for living virtuously: 2:20–21; 3:23; 4:18; 10:6, 16, 19; 12:7, 28; 16:17.

These passages can serve as a lens that brings selected facets of *The Odyssey* into a clear focus—doubly and triply so for a Christian reader.

Further Resources

In a special category is *Dictionary of Biblical Imagery*, edited by Leland Ryken and others (Downers Grove, IL: InterVarsity, 1998). Dozens of entries in this book provide collaborative reading from the Bible for motifs, themes, and archetypes in *The Odyssey*. In another special category are numerous books, some of them elaborate coffee-table books with photographs, that trace the geographic places in the Mediterranean region where the action of *The Odyssey* occurs. A representative of this copious genre is Robert Bittlestone, *Odysseus Unbound: The Search for Homer's Ithaca* (Cambridge, UK: Cambridge University Press, 2005).

Beye, Charles Rowan. *The Iliad, The Odyssey, and the Epic Tradition*. Garden City, NY: Anchor, 1966.

Clarke, Howard W. *The Art of The Odyssey*. Englewood Cliffs, NJ: Prentice-Hall, 1967.

Finley, John H., Jr. *Homer's Odyssey*. Cambridge, MA: Harvard University Press, 1978.

Griffin, Jasper. *Homer: The Odyssey*. Cambridge, UK: Cambridge University Press, 1987.

Lewis, C. S. *A Preface to Paradise Lost*. New York: Oxford University Press, 1942.

The early chapters of this book did more than anything else to rehabilitate the epic genre for modern readers.

Martin, Richard P. "Introduction." In *Homer: The Odyssey*. Translated by Edward McCrorie. Baltimore, MD: Johns Hopkins University Press, 2004.

Ryken, Leland. *Realms of Gold: The Classics in Christian Perspective*, chap. 1. Wheaton, IL: Harold Shaw, 1991.

Thalmann, William G. *The Odyssey: An Epic of Return*. New York: Twayne, 1992.

Tracy, Stephen V. *The Story of The Odyssey*. Princeton: Princeton University Press, 1990.

Young, Philip H. *The Printed Homer*. Jefferson, NC: McFarland, 2008.

Glossary of Literary Terms Used in This Book

Adventure story. An action-packed story of spectacular events, often (but not always) involving the fantastic.

Character/characterization. The persons and other agents who perform the actions in a story.

Dramatic irony. A situation in which the reader knows something that one or more characters in the work of literature do not know.

Epic. A long narrative poem in the high style; a species of hero story in which the hero embodies the ideals of the culture that produced a given epic.

Epithet. A title for a person or thing, such as "clever Odysseus" or "rosy-fingered dawn."

Fantasy. Literature that includes characters, settings, and events that do not exist in the real world.

Foil. Anything in a story (e.g., a character, plotline, or setting) that *sets off* something in the main story by being either a parallel or a contrast.

Genre. Literary type or kind, such as story or poem.

Hero story. A story that narrates the exploits of a central character who is largely (but not necessarily wholly) exemplary and whose experience is representative of people generally and the culture of the author specifically.

Heroic code; heroic ethos. A code of conduct that elevated military accomplishment to the highest value; heroes in this tradition were warriors motivated by the desire for fame, conquest, and rulership.

Myth; mythology. Strictly defined, a story about gods and goddesses but usually extended to cover stories in which there is a heavy incidence of the supernatural.

Narrative. Synonymous with story.

Plot. The carefully organized sequence of actions and events that make up a story, arranged as one or more conflicts that reach resolution.

Setting. The places where events in a story occur; can be temporal as well as physical.

Theme. An idea about life that is embodied in a work of literature and that can be deduced.

Travel story. A story built around a hero's journey to a succession of places.